State of a Union

The Half Century of Cameroon's Bicultural Experience

Emmanuel Yenshu Vubo

Langaa Research & Publishing CIG
Mankon, Bamenda

Publisher:
Langaa RPCIG
Langaa Research & Publishing Common Initiative Group
P.O. Box 902 Mankon
Bamenda
North West Region
Cameroon
Langaagrp@gmail.com
www.langaa-rpcig.net

Distributed in and outside N. America by African Books Collective
orders@africanbookscollective.com
www.africanbookcollective.com

ISBN: 9956-726-71-0

© Emmanuel Yenshu Vubo 2012

DISCLAIMER
All views expressed in this publication are those of the author and do not necessarily reflect the views of Langaa RPCIG.

In memory of late Joseph Temngah and late Etienne Njiki Bikoi,
University friends (who incidentally died at the same period) with whom we shared some of these ideas and ideals about Cameroon

Table of Contents

Preface.. v

Introduction.. vii

Chapter 1: Utopia and Disenchantment in the Making of the Bicultural Polity..1

Chapter 2: The Making of Ethnic Frontiers as Statecraft................... 33

Chapter 3: Language and the Linguistic Question in the Bicultural Project...53

Chapter 4: Between Assimilation and Roll Back in Harmonization Projects.. 79

Chapter 5: Towards the Anthropology of Conviviality and a Politics of Possibilities.. 105

References..145

Appendix I... 157

Appendix II..165

Preface

These critical reflections were first put in writing during the weekend of the 10th to the 12th of November 2006 in Strasbourg, then expanded upon during my stay of nearly two months in Besançon that covered the rest of November and December of the same year. At that period, I was preparing my pre-professorial qualification, the *Habilitation à Diriger des Recherches (HDR)*. The initial sketch was elaborated in parallel with the *Habilitation* and gradually developed into a post- HDR project as I discussed some of the issues with my tutor Professor Gilles Ferréol. This was in order as candidates in this research qualification have to analyze then own work but also to indicate projects on-going or for the future. With the completion of this work and its publication I have lived up to the promises that I made in the last but one chapter of my dissertation.

This work was also presented as a research project for funding and obtained a support grant within the Faculty Social and Management Sciences Research Grant Scheme of the University of Buea for 2008 to enable me continue and complete the research whose results are presented here. As such, this work is a natural conclusion of a tradition that I was initiated into within the French system of higher education professorships but which has had support from within the university where I work. I wish to thank my HDR tutor, Professor Gill Ferréol, for the initial encouragement and support to embark on this project. I also wish to express my gratitude to the Faculty which made the funds available.

Finally, I wish to acknowledge the numerous persons —all good-willed Cameroonians - with whom I have discussed these ideas over the years and who are just too many to enumerate here. I have dedicated the book to two friends who were the first person with whom I discussed the issues raised here. One was an Anglophone who taught in a Francophone university and the other was a Francophone with similar fortunes as he taught in an Anglophone university. This why this work is dedicated to their memory and what they symbolized as I have said of the first in the address during his posthumous honours reproduced in the appendix. Special mention will go to Mr Fred Ekane who painstakingly typed most of the manuscripts.

Buea, Wednesday, 2nd November 2011.

Introduction

Background

In 1961 the southern fragment of one of the territories of the former German colony of Kamerun, which had been administered after the outcome of the First World War in association with the British colony of Nigeria under the name of Southern Cameroons, opted to join the newly independent French speaking Republic of Cameroon in a plebiscite organized by the United Nations Organisation on the 11th of February of that year. The events leading up to that plebiscite itself, the process of making arrangements for coexistence and the varying fortunes of the experiment in cohabitation between the peoples resulting from the process have been the object of intense political debate and an abundant literature of both a political and academic nature. The making of such an unexpected marriage between cultures in a context where technical developments to handle the impending complications of the association were not seriously analysed is both a puzzle and the result of a combination of seemingly contradictory drives. On the one hand, there was the utopianism of the pan-Kamerun experience projected by idealistic nationalists and later on the remote Pan-Africanist leitmotif that came to be grafted unto it by politicians. On the other hand, it was expediency and political calculation (Njeuma 1995). In the end it was the euphoria and idealism of the utopian dimension that sailed the experience through a warped experiment and an essentially distorted national unity and centralized state project. More still, the political dimensions of the experiment have been the source of either disenchantment bordering on dejection or a social fragmentation along the lines of limited and restricted political participation, varied forms of cultural integration and varying degrees of social cleavages/tensions to the extent that it has become a very topical issue. While the unitarian vision - not to be confused with the centrist vision of the state as championed by the Ahidjo and Biya regimes - continues to take the idealized notion of a united country as a given or foregone conclusion that should not be challenged because of its primordial sanctity[1], there are restive voices being raised about the unitary form of the state and

---

[1] This takes as its starting point the Kamerun idea of the UPC.

the situation of Anglophones within that entity. These dissenting voices come from the Anglophone community but are also echoed by many good willed persons across the linguistic divide (Konings and Nyamnjoh 2003: 153 - 161). These are reflected in a variety of intellectual discourses that range from professed academic writings in social disciplines (sociology, law, history, political science, economics) and pamphlets of creative writing that express the discontent of the Anglophones as a community. Suffice it to say that the scope of this literature that started with political opening in the 1990s lays bare the shaky nature of the political arrangements between the two communities (see Konings and Nyamnjoh ibid.). A leading creative writer of the Anglophone movement, the late Bate Besong, considered the "Anglophone Cameroonian's existence [as] the burning question of the day" (1993: 15) because

> "The surrounding concentric rings of this smouldering infernal canyon may embrace a multitude of other victims in the present Cameroonian reality, but there is no doubt that our people, subjected to perpetual mental and psychological servitude, are the story-book victims of a cultural holocaust" (ibid.: 16)

He goes on to indicate that "... three decades have wrought for us: feudal oppression, mountains of suspicion and hate, retrogression, post-Foumban pauperisation, resentment" and treats the national unity project as "dubious and fragile" (ibid.). He calls for the writer to be nurtured by a style which he thinks has to be "artistically profound and politically correct: he can write works of indictment and works that show how [the writer's world] is and could be" (ibid: 18).

If there is anything as Anglophone political activism then that activism finds its most vocal expression in the intellectual community probably because its motto is "The Argument and not the Argument of Force". That explains why if anyone has been active in giving form to the Anglophone question, it has been a number of intellectuals. Prominent among these is Barrister Gorji Dinka whose call for a new social order represents an intellectual precursor in the analyses of the problem. Two university lecturers, Simon Munzu and Carlson Anyangwe, and a lawyer, Barrister Ekontang Elad, were instrumental in rallying support among the elite of the Anglophone community to the Anglophone cause through the organization of the All Anglophone Conferences (I, II, III) and drumming popular support as a response to the constitutional revision exercise of the first half of the 1990s. The development of an umbrella association, the SCNC - albeit its clandestine status -, owes much to this intellectual input. The factions that have developed out of this highly intellectualised and elitist movement also follow the lines of intellectual disagreement over the line of action to be taken. One evident effect of this development is the inability of this movement to penetrate to the grassroots as it has remained an intellectualised movement more preoccupied with legalistic arguments than with real issues and actions that touch the common man. That may explain why it is overtaken in its own sectional claims by ethno-regional movements which run counter to and are instrumental in undercutting its base (Konings and Nyamnjoh 2000, 2003). Although it can be considered as a sectional movement with clearly legitimate claims, this movement seems to be overshadowed by claims having their roots in a much deeper past (Yenshu 2003, 1998).

The majority of studies related to this problem have either been strictly judgmental in a value-laden direction or are scarcely an appraisal of the fortunes of this experience per se. The judgmental approach which sets out to articulate the problems of the English-speaking peoples of Cameroon in the main or to refute by diluting them in the general problematic of the social development of Cameroon is characteristic of scholars across the linguistic divide as well as non-Cameroonian scholars. English-speaking scholars are often given to apologias of all sorts as they seek to articulate the problems of their community, taking the problematic of the polity projected as a social and intellectual imperative. This trend appears in studies of both an historical and sociological nature (Konings and Nyamnjoh 1997, 2000, 2003; Nyamnjoh 1996; Awasom 1998, 2004; Chem-Langhee 1995, 1997; Jua and Konings 2004). In the debate one would find intra-systemic critics and the apologists or intellectual polemicists of English-speaking extraction.

Although scholarship on the "Anglophone problem" is rare within the French-speaking intellectual community, the little that exists tends to down play the crisis of the presence of the English-speaking community in Cameroon (Nkoum-me-Ntseny, 1996a and b, 1999; Melone, Minkoa-She and Sindjoun 1996; Menthong 1996, Sindjoun 1996; Ngamassu 2005). The rare studies in the English-speaking intellectual community which follow this trend, which is paradoxically very evident within pro-regime English-speaking politicians (Mbuagbo 2002) tend to engage in an essentially political discourse by laying blames for failures (Ngoh 1999, 1990, 2004, 2011). In this dialectics of accusation the intellectual community has become not only part of the debate but rather its main protagonists. As such, instead of shedding light on unfolding phenomena, they rather obscure the phenomena by their posture of intellectuals. With no end in view within the debate there is no advancement in understanding and thus no possibility of assisting in solving some of the problems arising out of the situation of cohabitation.

Appraisal studies are scarce and are now almost an issue of the past. The pioneering works of Johnson (1970), Le Vine (1971), Benjamin (1972), Bayart (1978) and Kofele-Kale (1980) have remained reference points but the evaluative dimension is largely missing in current studies. Monographs of the sort published by Nyamnjoh (1995), Nkwi and Nyamnjoh (1997), and Konings and Nyamnjoh (2003) document some of the political dimensions of the crisis from an Anglophone perspective but remain mute on the global experience. The aim of this study is to investigate the bicultural nation-state project from a multidimensional perspective. Such a study is significant for a number of reasons. For one reason, the Cameroon experience is an extremely unique one. Although it is not the only such living experience it is unique in its own way. One can find other multicultural experiences with which it is wrongly compared. These are the European experiences of Switzerland, Spain, Belgium and Luxemburg, and the North American experience of Canada with which it shares some striking similarities such as official multilingualism in English and French. However, these experiences differ from the Cameroonian experience in both conditions of genesis and historical depth. As such, the technologies and strategies for managing the multicultural differences are markedly different at the current stage. While the European and Canadian experiences reflect the histories of emergence of international competition and arrangements within the budding nationalisms of Europe, the Cameroonian experience is the result of pure chance whose unintended consequences were never analysed by architects.

Some analysts of the history of Cameroon will be surprised at the latter statement but that is the stark truth. Between 1949 and 1961 when the reality of the bicultural project became evident none of the politicians ever stopped to evaluate the consequence of an eventual bicultural experience. This is true of the utopian unionists of the Union des Populations du Cameroun (UPC) as of the entire Anglophone political class who were (notwithstanding the divergences) all originally committed to the Pan-Kamerun idea. This is true of E.M.L. Endeley's K.N.C., Foncha's K.N.D.P. and Ntumazah/Mukong's One Kamerun (extreme left-wing movement) as of the opportunists of Ahihjo's Union Camerounaise after the UPC was outlawed. It was not until after the plebiscite, which hinged more on the desire to leave a sour association experience with Nigeria - presented by pro-unionist politicians as infernal -, that the complications of the union experience began to dawn on architects. Things were more complicated than could be thought of the more so as these territories were coming out of a colonial experience that left them only with rudimentary means to handle the post-colonial situation in an autonomous manner. As such, besides having to cope with the ordinary problems of nation-building and habitual concerns of development, the new experience placed on its architects the additional burden of biculturalism in modern western cultures. Another such union on the continent, namely that of Tanganyika and Zanzibar, did not have such an additional burden to cope with.

From a broader perspective, the modern experience of nation-building has not been in the main one of maintaining and managing the difference. The main European models from which countries of the South take or try to mimic were originally assimilationist or uniformizing both in cultural and linguistic aspects. The experience has always been one of a dominant, hegemonic culture imposing its model on competing cultures. As such, the French achieved a unified language and culture only by adopting strategies that replaced a variety of competing models in the regions (e.g. Brittany, Basque country) or assimilated territories acquired through hegemonic ambitions (Alsace-Lorraine, Nice, Savoy). In like manner, the idea of "melting-pot" in American parlance meant moulding other cultural groups into the dominant model rather than the official endorsement of troubling alternatives. As such, territories acquired from France (Louisiana) or Spain (California, New Mexico, Texas) ceased to officially maintain their former French or Spanish identities. Even in Canada some enclaves of French extraction other than Quebec also simply assimilated into the English speaking community. The question of plural national coexistence has only become a more recent development both at policy level and in academia as evident in the interest and promotion of multiculturalism[2]. Even the

---

[2] In this regard see a critical analysis of multiculturalism by Michel Wievorka (2001) and Poutignat and Strieff-Fernat (1996).

questions raised are more concerned with other aspects of difference (race, ethnicity defined variously, sub-nationalities) with the model of cultural and linguistic monopoly and dominance left unchallenged. The choice therefore of a bicultural and bilingual project by the architects of Cameroon's independence was therefore a rare fact whose full consequences were not obvious to them.

This small book plans to revisit the genesis and history of the union in order to understand the particular factors which have been at the basis of the union. It will start with an in-depth analysis of the politics of integration within the bicultural project and experience (politico-administrative and elite strategies as well as collective responses whether by state agents or by ordinary citizens; strategies of inclusion and integration as well as the responses of partial integration, accommodation and rejection that operate at all levels). Related to this is the is the issue of the economy of attachment to the polity that are an important dimension in integration: history of economic integration (state institutions, monetary issues, parastatal companies), the development of business communities across the linguistic divide, the job market and working conditions, connectivity (communication routes, the language of business), population movements and the urban economies, rural development and the global of spatial development which places a premium on constructing (or enabling) gigantic urban centres as against rural enclaves and dwarfed colonial towns reduced to the status of second and third rate administrative centres. The analysis of the economy of contact will target the lines of bifurcation, ambivalence and the intensity of contact and interaction whether in conflict, acculturation or accommodation.

The hope is to equally examine issues related to global cultural, political and economic trends: cultural trends, membership in global organization reflecting colonial history (Commonwealth of Nations, Organisation de la Francophonie), the increasing weight of uniform acts on the *de facto* one-state-two-systems approach through sub-regional projects that reflect colonial historical legacies and continuing neo-colonial trends (CEMAC, CIMA Code, COBAC). I will thus target official strategies (Ahidjo's neutrality, Biya's equilibrium approach) but also developments that express a drift towards participating in strategies that integrate Cameroon into its unique Francophone environment and demonstrate how these impact on internal processes. Conversely, we may also observe cultural, demographic and economic developments that point to the Anglicisation of the French component in an officious and almost imperceptible manner as a result of the presence of the Anglophone component. These processes transcend borders in the immediate proximity of Nigeria to the West but are also transnational when Francophones are interested in the English world in general. In the same manner the English speaking territory also becomes a transit point between the English speaking world and Francophone Cameroon (and, beyond that, Central Africa as a whole) either officially or otherwise. These multiple processes are evident but are largely unreported in the literature and would thus need to be explored to understand the complexity of their structures and the multiplicity of forces at work.

Focus in the second chapter is on the geopolitics of coexistence with its corollary of ethno-regionalism. Instead of the Anglophone problem we will rather devote a special section to the crisis of the Anglophone presence in the ethno-regional craftsmanship that has been at the basis of statecraft in Cameroon since colonial times. This will explain how the Anglophone component of the polity has been progressively integrated into what has been "ethnicised" although it was a constitutional entity that had joined Cameroon through what Alain Finkelraut termed an elective process. In this way, it has fitted rather oddly into what Konings and Nyamnjoh (2003) have termed a political arithmetic that tends to eclipse its cultural specificity.

In examining the language situation and the linguistic question at the centre of the bicultural experience in chapter three we hope to target official strategies of managing the situation but also popular responses in situations of difference. Official strategies targeted are official enactments (constitution, law, official directives) and the school system (official training in second languages at all levels) but also effectiveness and the resultant effects which may not be same. Are there effects of imposition or real practice of two languages? If there is effectiveness, who are those likely to practice the two languages and at what level? What have been the trends over history and what are the likely trends towards the future? In short, we will be exploring official action and reaction to it. However, we will go beyond this to also examine what obtains outside the administration and the formal sector, namely in popular social interactions and informal economic exchange. These are the spaces of various forms of creative mixing that put the situation of Cameroon as one ranging between what Jean-Loup Amselle calls "*logiques métisses*" ([1990]2009), official bilingualism and various forms of multilingualism.

Another dimension that will be studied will be the official arrangements of coexistence. On the one hand we hope to examine the processes of harmonisation in a variety of domains (education, administration, the armed forces and police, justice) in chapter four. The hypothesis in this regard is that their fortunes in each sphere are rather varied. Some trends point to the spaces of imposition of a francophone model (not to be confused with a French model) and *"frenchification"* of public life through organisation, operation and learning in French as may be the case with the administration, the armed and the police. In education, history points to rather hesitant attempts at harmonisation. The judiciary presents a picture of practices ranging from harmonisation of most of its key aspects (administrative organisation of magistracy, legislation, investigation, sanction) by streamlining them to the dominant politico-administrative structure which itself has been built along the system develop in the former colony of French Cameroons, harmonious blends (the recent criminal procedure code, the bar association) and maintenance of procedural differences. The operation of the system in two linguistic spaces does not abstract significantly from this logic. As such, the overall picture is a plural mix of assimilated spaces, a few harmonised patches and continuing exclusive mono-cultural spaces. We hope to examine the degree to which each of the process is at work in Cameroon.

In the last chapter I finally hope to explore in detail the anthropology of conviviality within the polity. This will start with an examination of certain models of integration which will enable us to describe and analyse the situations of conviviality. With reference to specific case studies and situations, I will examine both elite and popular forms of conviviality which I consider ambivalent because they oscillate between cross-fertilisation and rejection, low-intensity conflicts over ascendancy and intense interactions/acculturations. This is a process of cultivating differences, the development of stereotypes/typifications at the same time that everyone is striving to live the same Cameroonian nationality. It is a bifurcated national identity which is lived as normal without this constituting either a situation of ambivalence or contradiction. This will be accompanied by proposals for a way forward. The appendices, made up of a series of articles that were published in *The Post* during the 1990s and a tribute during the funeral of one of the friends with whom these ideas were developed, will throw more light on how these ideas have been nurtured. The tribute portrays the staggering attempts by Anglophones intellectuals to find their place in the bicultural polity.

Chapter One

Utopia and Disenchantment in the Making of the Bicultural Polity

The Genesis: Between Utopia, Immature Politicking and Political Opportunism

The birth of the bicultural polity of Cameroon is one of those surprising twists of history that took hardly twelve years to become a reality. No one could predict (and indeed no one did predict) that the tiny section of the German colony of Kamerun, which had been attached to the Eastern Region of the British protectorate of Nigeria after the First World War, would ever become part of an independent country in association with a French speaking component at independence. In fact, the "natural" tendency was for the League of Nations and, later on, United Nations mandate countries (Britain and France) to administer the territories with a view to integrating them into their colonial empires and later on spheres of influence.

While the British administered its own discontinuous territories of Northern and Southern Cameroons to become part of a gigantic Nigeria and made no secret of doing so (Ngoh 1990), the French closely associated its territory with the Afrique Equatoriale Francaise (AEF) with which it shared a common colonial community (notably in administrative and financial terms). Both administering authorities practiced the same cultural policies of replacing the earlier German influences (language, administrative culture) with theirs and proceeded to modify the external boundaries of their territories to suit their colonial designs. As a result, part of what constituted the part of the Kamerun territory inherited by France were chipped off and added to its colonies of Oubangui-Shari, Tchad, Congo-Brazzaville and Gabon. In like manner, some cosmetic boundary adjustments undertaken by the British in the late 1940s annexed tiny parts of Southern Cameroons to Nigeria. These adjustments created a situation whereby by the time the independence became an urgent issue of debate a combination of the mandated territories did no more reflect the original German Kamerun territory because it had been redesigned to reflect the intentions of the administering powers to integrate the territories into their respective colonial and (subsequently) neocolonial spheres of influence. Such a policy was also actively pursued in areas where some such partitions had taken place as in the case of Togo where the French replaced German with French as language of operation and culture while the British integrated its own sphere into Ghana. Moreover, in either sphere the administering power actively sought to contain any pro-German Pan-Kamerun idea (Austen and Derrick 1996; Derrick 1989; Amazee 2003). How did the bicultural polity then come about?

Such a question looks absurd when official narratives of this process are almost common place. The historical facts are related in history text books and in scientific journals almost in a habitual manner such that the facts look self-evident but the forces that underlie these facts are completely ignored. Psychology-based studies that place a lot of premium on personalities involved in the process ignore the current of opinion and collective social movements that were at play at both local and global level. If the latter are taken into consideration, then one will attribute the genesis of the polity to the growth of utopian populist nationalism in French Cameroons in response to overt French colonial repression (Joseph 1977). This utopianism was adopted by a political class of Southern Cameroon disenchanted within a colonial Nigerian federation which dwarfed their individual aspirations and became the leitmotif for the movement away from any negotiated association with Nigeria as the collective attitude of this political class reflected a tendency towards manipulation, obstinacy (see appendix 1) and a disregard for realism. The third factor is the ability of utopian nationalists or unionists to play on the budding non-alignment movement of the Bandung initiative and the communist block countries during the UN debates on the plebiscite question which did not take into consideration the operational/practical implications of the union option. Lastly, the late appropriation of the nationalist programme by the Ahidjo group after the UPC was outlawed and when the union option had become almost an imperative in the French Cameroons partly explains the success of the unification idea. As in the other cases, this expedient step did not also take into consideration the practical implications. As such, the making of the polity was the result of utopian populism, political miscalculations and obstinacy and thoughtless recuperation by politicians ill-prepared to lead even a mono-cultural entity.

It is however worth noting from a *systemic dimension* that none of these factors taken alone could have made for the historic choice that ushered in the bicultural nation-state project. Nor was the combination of the factors alone likely to have resulted in the situation without the enabling conditions: these enabling conditions were provided by the time frame of independence, the imperatives of the international situation and the nature of the inter-state system in the post-World War II situation. If one proceeds from the conditions to the factors and then to the effects then one is more likely to obtain better results than if one were looking for effects on their own as if these effects could produce themselves. In the immediate aftermath of the Second World War decolonisation had become an imperative imposed on the world system of capitalism by the shattering effects of the war. Colonial powers such as Britain and France that revelled in colonial empire-building and that had not envisaged giving up their colonies for any reason were soon forced by the circumstances and the new institution of multilateral management of the world system (namely the UN) – not without the influence of the United States of America[1] - to give up their colonial possessions in the name of decolonisation. The average time frame (15 years after the end of the war) or the range (between four for countries like India and sixteen for most French African countries) point to a rather *hurried process*, the more so as decolonisation was on no agenda before the outbreak of the war. This explains the complications that suddenly arose within colonial administrations but also the local peoples responses to the situation. It is this opening provided by the international situation that explains the emergence of the independence movements and its "leaders" who were not the same types of personalities everywhere. In other words, the clamour for independence was not at all a totally independent endeavour of the local peoples. It was rendered possible only by the shift in international attitudes as the colonial powers were shattered by the fortunes of the war and the decline of Europe into sub-imperial status under the watershed or shelter of the United States.

Moreover, although there were ideological divergences in the emerging context of the Cold War that had not yet achieved its full contours, both the United States and the Soviet block achieved consensus on the question of decolonisation and had made it an imperative at the level of the UN. There were divergences only as to who will be the beneficiaries of the decolonisation process and the postcolonial situation. Was decolonisation to benefit the Western capitalist block or was it to add to the growing spectrum of countries claiming a Soviet communist model? All local champions of the independence cause were circumscribed within the logic of this context and had to cope with this dilemma. The emergence of the Bandung initiative of

---

[1] Cf. in this regard, Nwaubani (2003).

Non-Alignment was a way out but only after the countries had achieved formal independence. From the point of view of the Western block countries in the emerging *bipolar scheme*, independence was to be a substitution of forms of intervention where what was later styled neo-colonialism would be but a generalized form of *Greater Indirect Rule*: independence within the same sphere of influence of the colonial metropolis. One can understand De Gaulle's open stance in this light but Britain and other colonial powers operated within the same frame. The paradox is that some countries that opted out of this perspective had to lean towards the Soviet block which postured as the champion of radical emancipation from capitalism in a posture it styled progressive. Apprehensions about such likelihood therefore arose within colonial political circles when independent-looking anti-colonial movements arose. Invariably, such an option was met with repression as any movement branded as communist was immediately considered anathema in the colonies. In other words, persons who chose an alternative model of independence were also to run into conflict with the colonial administrations which had envisaged independence only as a formal process.

The Union des Populations du Cameroun (UPC) opted precisely out of this model of formal independence by not *playing the game* which could have consisted of merely creating structures that *would simply take over*. It instead seized the opportunity offered by the shift in international climate to challenge France's right to treat Cameroon as a colony when it was not. Its dialectical thrust was not only to have claimed independence for Cameroon as any other political formation would have done and got it on a competitive basis organized by the colonial and decolonising power. In purely logical terms that are true of ideological formulations, the UPC argued that Cameroon was greater than French Cameroons and that the territories under UN mandate be granted independence at once and collectively. That is the substance of the twin claims of immediate independence and unification. This was obviously oblivious of the modifications that had been made on the territories by the governing colonial powers[2]. The UPC ideologues in this regard were stating in other terms what Sekou Touré would say later in 1958 but went beyond that to speak for peoples whom they had not addressed. I style this form of unionism idealistic because it made a nationalist claim

---

[2] The territory which the Southern Cameroons would eventually join was a much reduced entity because the "French abrogation of the Franco-German treaty of 1911…[which] had extended the boundary of Southern [Kamerun] to the South of Spanish Guinea" (Ngoh 2011: 2). By this token, the dream of the unionists did not include all of German Kamerun.

about peoples who had never been a nation (hardly thirty years of German ineffective control of a vast territory). Moreover, it was utopian because it did not evaluate the practical implications of the eventual outcome of the project it was heralding. To the proponents it was enough for the sake of the argument and in so doing they were taking the "things of logic for the logic of things" as Bourdieu would have it. Other options could have been for the UPC to end at challenging French rights to rule the mandated territory as a colony. They were, however, lured into this form of idealization and utopia by the apparent freedoms that were enjoyed within the British administered territories but which were in effect the effect of benign neglect as the territories were left to the whims and caprices of the claimants to ethnic hegemony within the respective regions to which they were attached in the logic of indirect rule (namely the Ibo for the Eastern Region, the Yoruba in the Western Region and the Hausa-Fulani for the Northern Region). In this regard, one can rightly say that utopian vision and idealism was generated by an inaccurate perception of certain colonial realities. Such idealizations have survived till date and would explain the fervour and enthusiasm with which the union experience is lived by certain Cameroonians of French speaking experience.

If the French mandate experience was driving the UPC into a Pan-Kamerun ideal and utopia which would benefit from the positive aspects of "British" culture, the political class of Southern Cameroons was driven into this utopian ideal by a form of Indirect Rule wherein the British had given free hand to the Igbo to make a claim to ascendancy within the Eastern Region of its colony of Nigeria. In such a scheme it was not the British who were in control; it was the Igbo who were in control for the British. The abuses committed by the Igbo were therefore local abuses but whose benefits went to the British. This was the very essence of Indirect Rule through a settler experience as would be observed elsewhere in the British Empire: the use of proxy irrespective of its abuses. Secondly, the articulation of Nigerian politics around three hegemonic entities (Ibo, Yoruba, Hausa-Fulani) with no place for subgroups such as the Southern Cameroons tended to alienate the political class which had been involved in competitive politics since the late 1940s.

These factors made the association with French Cameroons an attractive alternative to consider. It has to be noted that despite the restrictions on colonial frontiers and the nationalist uprising on the French side – which was more of a vast campaign of anti-foreigner terror concentrated in "Bamileke" country, the Mungo area and Bassaland –, cross border population movements into the French were considerable compared with movement to Nigeria which were restricted by Igbo monopoly of opportunities in the Eastern Region. In fact, French Cameroons had the image of a land of opportunities to peoples from the adjacent Western Grassfields and the whole corridor of the demarcation line right to the coast despite its insecurity. If one were to talk of insecurity (presented at the time by the colonial power as terrorism), it was for foreigners especially settler colonists in the Mungo in particular and some urban areas. Reports point to Nkongsamba, Manjo, Loum and Douala as poles of attraction to immigrants from the adjacent Southern Cameroons much more than Enugu, Calabar or Lagos. One would have expected that such immigrants were not subjected or subject to the same type of treatment as indigenes of French Cameroons. These movements were accompanied in the reverse direction by the movement of peoples from adjacent French administered territory into English administered territory in search of opportunities. One has to note that although hard labour had led to an earlier wave of natives of the French speaking territories in the 1920s (Epale 1975) and political instability accounted for some population movements of some considerable dimensions, the larger proportion of movements in the colonial period was in search of opportunities (new settlements, new urban centres, new plantations, new industrial sites). Such movements and the resulting human intercourse account for the spread of the ideals and their potential to gain grounds within the new political class. Arguments about trans-border affinities were only fostered by such developments. This was facilitated by the fact that Pidgin English and not any of the two official languages of the mandate powers was the lingua franca of this category of moving and intensely interacting peoples all along the axis we have mentioned before. As such, the much vaunted cross border fraternity found its geographical and anthropological limits within this region. When the budding political class adopted them it was more of adopting an urban creed but it also did so in an uncritical manner. A British official, Foley Newns had warned that the KNDP was incompetent to appreciate the issues involved" whereas the "people on the other side [were] more sophisticated" (in Ngoh 2011: 25). In this regard, it was oblivious of the geographically limited applicability of the ideals and its inherent problems. Initially it was the original slogan for an alternative away from Nigeria for the KNC but it soon degenerated simply into a mere stake in the game of competitive politics as the only form of politics the Southern Cameroons group was used to. In fact, schooling in politics as the search for alternative solutions to the same collective interest was missing. The politicians understood politics only as competition for power in itself (see appendix 1).

By the time this became concrete as the two alternatives it was clear that the utopian vision had won because it was the main issue and not the alternative. Surprisingly, a minority extremist faction of this utopian vision in the Southern Cameroons, in this case the One Kamerun (OK) party, had succeeded to lobby both the Soviet block and the emerging Bandung movement to force through these alternatives at the core of the 1961 plebiscite at the level of the United Nations, thus undercutting British expectations of having to grant independence in normal fashion within the status quo. Unfortunately, by the time the plebiscite was conducted neither the UPC nor its OK allies were in a position to benefit from the outcome of the elections. It has to be understood that the union option presented itself principally as the most viable option to UPC nationalists opposed to the colonial regime in the French Cameroons (repression set in immediately after the UPC was created in 1948) and to a Southern Cameroons political class wary of the domineering attitude of the Igbo in the Eastern region of Nigeria where they occupied a dominant position. This is irrespective of the gains of quasi-regional status and the promise of full regional status in Nigeria that was never objectively evaluated and exploited. Instead, the union with French Cameroons had suddenly become the overarching argument pitted against arguments of gains or promises of further gains.

When Ahidjo become internal Premier in 1958 he appropriated this utopian vision too by talking of independence and unification although that was not in his original scheme. This change in position should not be taken for real but as out of pure expediency as this was meant to empty the UPC of their populist discourses centred on the same themes. This was the more so as the UPC had been outlawed and some of its members were driven underground or simply assassinated as in the case of Um Nyobe. In short, it was just one of the ways of undercutting the radical nationalists and occupying centre stage ideologically since he had occupied the dominant position politically. However his version of unionism was radically different from that of UPC and the Southern Cameroons politicians who had converted it into the principal question of competitive politics. It had to wait to find full expression only after the plebiscite of 11 February 1961. At best, Ahidjo's attitude can be considered as one of opportunism but one which he would later combine with repression and manipulation to usher into his own practical version of the union.

Asymmetrical Negotiations, Inconclusive Arrangements and Forced Political Order

In the new circumstances, how the union became possible (its initiating and constituting acts) did not more concern all who had bought the idea. Firstly, the form which it took was very far removed from the UPC claim which was not simply granted because this would have been tantamount to abdication on the part of the colonial administration. As a plebiscite question, it was narrowed down to the English-speaking territories whose fate its Southern politicians had succeeded to graft and associate to its competitive politics. In this way, the exclusion of the essential stake holders, namely the UPC and other political parties in the French Cameroons, from a wider debate resulted in unintended outcomes. Secondly, the UN decision to narrow down the plebiscite to the two territories of Northern and Southern Cameroons compromised the destinies of these territories by annexing them either to the future of French Cameroons or Nigeria who were not themselves requested to make the same options either to accept or refuse the decisions coming out of the consultations[3]. This would later explain the difficulties of the politicians of the ex-Southern Cameroons in being able to negotiate other options after the plebiscite and the ensuing arrangements between the contracting parties. None of the contending parties in Southern Cameroons had envisaged that the elections would take the form of a *fait accompli* association when once they were over. The impression that the issue of a union would be a continuous debate or recurrent plebiscite as in the case of competitive politics would turn out to be entirely erroneous. Lastly, when the die of association with French Cameroons was cast with the results of the plebiscite in Southern Cameroons, two sets of actors were left with an idea they never generated - Southern Cameroonian politicians and Ahidjo's *Union Camerounaise* (largely an outgrowth of the "Bloc du Nord") – and in peculiarly troubling circumstances (the resort of the UPC to armed struggle, the rise to power of an Ahidjo regime through French manipulation, rising

---

[3] Ngoh (2011: 15) rather insists on the fact that "people of French Cameroons were never asked, in whatever form or form, if they wanted reunification with British Southern Cameroons or with any part of British Cameroons". This question should hold too for Nigeria from the standpoint of self-determination.

authoritarianism, political repression, restriction of liberties) (see Ateba Yene 1988; Wonyu 1985; Mongo Beti 2003). The unionists had won the elections as expected but not in the circumstances that suited the idealism of the initiators of this utopian current. In the spirit of competitive politics they had simply won and were bent on continuing in such a spirit. Reality did not even dawn on this group right up till the time they were sidelined within new versions of competitive politics that placed greater premium on positioning within the new polity.

The federal arrangement that came out of the Foumban talks was meant more to put a hold the ex-Southern Cameroons from adding to the political weight of the South against the North as did informal arguments between Foncha and Ahidjo (Konings and Nyamnjoh 2003 :12-13). It is interesting to note that this arrangement lasted just practically as the task of pacifying the Southern part of French-speaking Cameroon lasted. It is also common knowledge that this federal arrangement was undercut by various forms of centralist policies and arrangements, relegation of West Cameroon to regional status within the Federal Republic through Decree No. 61-DF-15 of 15 December 1961 (less than two months into the union)[4], and institution of offices (federal inspectors to regions) whose powers undercut those of the Prime Minister of West Cameroon, these resulting in what Ngoh (2011: 31) has called "a centralized federation". All these appear to many a scholar as cosmetic rather conjunctional measures. That is far from it. In what he styles the "constitutional problem" resulting from the plebiscite Ahidjo was unequivocal when he stated that:

> What was the exact nature of the problem to be solved? To provide Reunification with institutions. The principle that difference of language and culture made a federal regime necessary *at the start* having been accepted, it was necessary to consecrate this unification legally by giving it a charter, in other words, by giving it a constitution.

But two other questions arose: was it necessary to draw up a constitution for the Federal Republic of Cameroon or was it preferable to amend the constitution of the then Cameroon Republic which had been approved by the people in the consultation of the 21st of February 1960?

---

[4] This is the forerunner of the ever-recurring dream of regionalism that has resurfaced after a long spate of Jacobin centralization when there were strong demands for several forms of autonomy. This gives the impression that Yaoundé is obsessed with this model.

The Cameroon Republic and the territory previously under British trusteeship constituted a single historic unit: the Cameroon Nation, a single moral unit: the Cameroon Fatherland. But on the other hand, they were too distinct political entities, on one side, an independent sovereign state possessing an international legal personality; on the other, a territory without a political, international status.

> It being unthinkable to tamper with the republican form of the regime, it was the republic which had to transform itself into a federation, *taking into account the return to it of part of its territory, a part possessing certain special characteristics the question therefore was not the of the birth of a new republic with a federal form.*

Bowing to this logic, we decided, therefore, to amend the constitution of the 21st of February 1960, since language and cultural difference needed to be given legal consideration. Thus, it was that, at the historic Foumban Conference. ....we announced the main outline of the modifications by which the constitution of the 21st February 1960 should become the constitution of the Federal Republic of Cameroon (Ahidjo 1964:23)[5]. (Emphasis added)

The extensive quote has been intended to make the point clear: the federalist form did not mean the same thing for Ahidjo's team and the winners of the Southern Cameroon's plebiscite ballot[6]. While the latter understood it to be a permanent arrangement of even a confederate nature, Ahidjo and his team treated it simply as a temporary measure ("at the start"), implying that other arrangements were possible. While the Southern Cameroons champions of unification believed in the status of a contracting party in a relationship, the Ahidjo group were posturing as the representatives of a historic nation who were playing an equally historic role of welcoming home prodigal sons. While the winners of the Southern

---

[5] In fact, this had always been Ahidjo's position. As early as May 1961, shortly before the Foumban conference, he had stated that the only option was "to revise the Constitution of the Republic of Cameroon…in order to allow for Southern Cameroons" (Ngoh 2011: 50).

[6] Ngoh (ibid.: 55) seems to share this view when he says that "underneath the surface, it was obvious that at the Foumban conference, Ahidjo and Foncha were not speaking the same language" but contradicts himself when he affirms immediately that "Foncha had accepted that amend the constitution of the Republic of Cameroon" (ibid.: 56).

Cameroons ballot were dreaming of a new constitution that would safeguard their interests in the new arrangement, Ahidjo's group openly talked of a simple amendment (a practice that has become the tradition ever since) that implied the equally simple grafting of Southern Cameroons to a fatherland proclaimed by its own self proclaimed father, Ahidjo himself ("therefrom to it of parts of its territory"). Instead of a consensual constitution voted from a conference the so-called federal constitution was a mere revision of the constitution of the French-speaking Republic of Cameroon). Taking recourse to the logic of the utopian nationalists, he sealed this union with words which have ever since been sacrosanct to his regime and its heirs: it was a "single historic", "moral unit" whose indivisibility was now but a matter of time. This is how a union dreamed of by idealists was born in what looked like a dialogue of the deaf but which in all respects was the product of asymmetrical understandings: each person came to the same table and went away with his or her own understanding of the resolutions without there being a consensus.

Ahidjo's regime evidently had other preoccupations to deal with which the unification question only came to complicate, namely the management of the ethno-regional equation in which his power base was challenged by both Southerner politicians and northern non-fulbe (Kirdi) elements and the lingering French presence in the aftermath of French Cameroons independence in the logic of the colonial party's determination to maintain relations over its former Empire beyond decolonization (Benot[1994]2001: 174). The management of the Anglophone equation in its federal form wherein the federated state of West Cameroon was relegated to the status of one of the regions and, later on, the dismantling of the federal scheme itself can be best understood in this light. Informal arrangements or cosmetic reminders in the form of token bilingualism (principally for English speaking Cameroonians) or the name of "United Republic" were but political gimmicks because the real intention was to integrate the ex-Southern Cameroons within Cameroon with no intentions of retracting. When Paul Biya, Ahidjo's constitutional successor, decided in 1984 to introduce a constitutional amendment which deleted the qualifier of "United" from the designation of Cameroon he thought he was dismantling Ahidjo's legacy of cosmetic concessions. On the contrary, he was in actual fact operating according to the same logic but this time in a more overt manner. "Integration" was decreed with a stroke of the pen to be the higher form or the ultimate endpoint of unity. Differences were considered to have ended and everyone became a citizen on his own right: no minority, no majority. The paradox is that new types of minorities and majorities have been defined to replace claims of the English speaking peoples to the status of a constitutional minority.

By this time all the architects of the union had lost touch with the unfolding developments. The UPC had been decapitated and, even when it spoke, the question of the union was no more its concern, preoccupied as it was with a governance-centred critique and the lingering neo-colonial presence of France in Cameroon. Most of the winners of the 1961 ballot were out of the way or were on their way out. Ahidjo himself had resigned and was having his own post-resignation problems with Biya. He eventually died in 1987 while Muna, who had become the official representative of the English speaking community since 1971(2) when he replaced Foncha as Number II person in government, was also thrown out of ruling circles by 1988. When Foncha made a lame claim to defend the English speaking community in a petition to President Biya in 1990 he was snubbed and no one could hear him. It was too late to undo the damage or reverse the consequences of what had resulted from the rather confused and muddled turn of events. What emerged from this situation can best be termed a *forced political order* in opposition to a *contractual relationship* that should normally underlie a democratic dispensation. Such a forced political order, which is largely the work of the Ahidjo regime but also maintained with key modifications by its successor, the Biya regime, is characterized by an insistence on:

1. Clearly and definitely closing the door to further debate on the bicultural question and, through it, the issue of the form of the state which is declared "One and Indivisible" forever, whatever complications must have arisen as a result of the union;

2. Treating the idea of the union as an unshakable given by giving the impression that the majority of those concerned are contented and actively support the union. As such, separatists or even campaigners for minority rights are treated as being in the minority and a hand-full of trouble makers (Biya in *Jeune Afrique* No. 1990 of 2 – 8 March 1999) while pro-regime elites of English-speaking extraction are occasionally mobilized to counter the influence of the former. This is reflected in the spirit of the debates leading to and eventual formulation of the constitutional revision exercise of the 1993-1993 years and culminating in the law of 18 January 1996 which treated

the question of the form of the state as a given with alternatives being only in regional decentralization (witness the return to Ahidjo's model of regionalism) and a warped protection of minorities that has become problematic in itself (Yenshu Vubo 2005, 2006).

On the contrary the premises of the forced political order are as illusory as the utopia of the original union idea. The English speaking community is restive as a substantial fraction of its elites denounces some of the abuses to which it is subjected. The state is not "One-and-Indivisible" as witnessed by the ethno-regional centrifugal forces that rocked its foundation during the early years of political effervescence in the early 1990s.

Dynamics of Chaotic Integration in a Forced Political Order

The illusion of the achievement of a consensual order obtained by force and manoeuvre is further belied by the chaos it has engendered through various global and sectional policies pursued in a distorted manner. By consenting to maintain a bicultural structure during the federal experiment and attempting to harmonise same only to abandon later on has a left a patchwork of de facto biculturalism (one-state-two-systems), partially harmonized structures and in some cases dangerous hybrids. This is the case of the school system, language, police and the judiciary which have evolved in this forward-and-backward movement. We will not delve into details here as this will be dealt within in later sections of this book.

The politics of force and manipulation has also engendered in its wake a fragmentary political situation within the English speaking community. Besides the generalized feeling of marginalisation that spares nobody even government officials and ministers, the community and its elites have been placed in a situation where they have to choose between being within the regime or against it. This fragmented attachment is indeed as old as the union itself or when disenchantment set in - and it indeed set in quite early. Such a situation resembles that of the vanquished in a war where the only alternatives are between accepting defeat or facing extermination. In fact, this is rather unfair. The choice for any people cannot be: accept or you are out. In the past this was the situation which led to imprisonment for late Albert Mukong and exile for Gorji Dinka, historic challengers of the Ahidjo's orchestrated forced political order. It is the situation at the basis of inclusion or exclusion of English speaking politicians in government. Those who support are in and those who are even just critical are out. In more recent circumstances this bifurcated acceptance has been extended to imply a cleavage between North Westerners (considered as opposing and out) and South Westerners (considered pro-regime and in). Even then, the extent of cooptation has dwindled to its most symbolic and token level: a Prime Minister with merely supervisory powers over government and few junior cabinet positions out of proportion with its size of two fifth of the population. The general history of this trend will explain the rise of separatism and generalized discontent as well as explain the radical reaction of Anglophone civil society organizations, the media and the intelligentsia.

Within the teaming chaos characterized by distorted policies where progress is undone by regressive policies, stagnation or lack of action emerges an atmosphere where Cameroonians are living the situation of forced political order in tensions, accommodation, exclusion, hybrids, adaptations, ignorance, rejection, abandonment etc each in his own way. It is this highly complex situation that Cameroonians have inherited today.

The Spatial Human Dimension: Population Movements and the Economy

I indicated in an earlier section that the Pan-Kamerun ideal was facilitated by cross-border movements in the colonial period and that these were bi-directional and reciprocal. Such trends were facilitated in one case by colonial repression and forced labour in the French administered sphere and the search for opportunities and the Igbo scare in the English. This explains the existence of substantial colonies of each territory on the other side of the symmetry that date to the colonial period. As such, one would find "settlers" from the present North West and South West provinces in the present Mungo division and Douala, on the one hand, and, on the other, descendants of people from the present Centre (Eton, Akonolinga, Ewondo), Western (Bamum, Bamileke) and Littoral (Duala, Bassa, Bakoko, Pongo, Abo) provinces with roots far back into the colonial period (see Epale 1975: 116) particularly in the South West Province (Delancey 1974: 193 -198). These peoples and their descendants have adopted the official languages of their milieu and actually do not feel the presence of returning to their original homes. It is likely that the period of the federal experiment did not witness a lot of movements due to the political framework which tended to keep peoples apart but movements to important poles of attraction such as Douala or the Mungo were substantial if one goes by oral reports.

It is the advent of the unitary state and the post – 1972 referendum experience that led to massive cross-border movements. The most important of these movements were directed towards Yaoundé and Douala as important job markets for youngsters and civil servants of English-speaking origins. Bafoussam, Nkongsamba and other towns of the Mungo later on became important poles of attraction. Conversely, Bamenda (for immigrants from the neighbouring Western province) and Kumba were principal poles of attraction for both their hinterlands and Francophone areas. Limbe (formerly Victoria) became an important pole of attraction for Francophone immigrants especially after the National Petroleum Refinery (SONARA) was established in its vicinity in the late 1970s. The administrative practice of posting persons to work in areas others than their original homelands has also accounted for some degree of immigrant settlements but seems not to be significant.

These developments occurred at a time when the towns were expanding especially in the French speaking territory. Douala and Yaoundé have witnessed a phenomenal growth since then until they constitute megalopolises that concentrate more than a quarter of the country's population. Bamenda and Bafoussam have also become gigantic metropolises far beyond their sizes of the 1970s. The same was true of Kumba and Nkongsamba for some time but there appears to be stagnation at some point. If other towns have expanded in population size (as is the case of Garoua, Maroua, Ngaoundere, Kumbo, Bafang, Edea, Bertoua, Ebolowa, Sangmelima) they have benefited more from the administrative push which projected them into centres of government[7]. The rest of the towns have sort of stagnated especially when they are cut off from the important centres of decision making by lack of good transport networks (e.g. Wum, Nkambe, Mamfe, Banyo, Mbalmayo, Betare Oya, Mbengwi) or when there are no important services or industrial plants. The Mungo area remains a past pole of attraction of migrant labour in the agricultural sector and continues to attract a considerable amount of immigrants as this is a sort of Fertile Crescent. The overall picture is one of two vast emerging megapolises seconded by tottering secondary metropolises and urban centres, on the one

---

[7] Buea has only benefited from the introduction of the university although its development is limited by space and topography.

hand, and a vast hinterland which they draw from in terms of rural exodus and food supply, on the other. I have hinted to the problematic of this highly imbalanced model of development in general (Yenshu 1997).

These population movements have sent the English-speaking community far and wide into the French-speaking territory in the South of the country with the highest concentrations being in Douala and Yaoundé, obvious reasons being size of job market and imperatives of administration, and Bafoussam (proximity factor). The presence of Francophones is also significant in some important towns of Anglophone Cameroon such as Bamenda, Buea, Limbe and Tiko and Kumba and hardly goes beyond to the other towns. Such a situation thus reflects an unequal movement across the divide with more English-speaking peoples moving into the French-speaking section than is the reverse. It would be significant to conduct a survey of the type of activities that attract these movements to also determine the degree of qualitative imbalance. An observation, which could still be considered hypothetical for the movement, is that an East-West (Francophone-Anglophone) movement is concentrated in the lucrative segments of the modern sector (economy, public service) such as command positions in the administration, management positions in some parastatals (SONARA), involvement in all levels of commerce (petty trade and wholesale), investment in extractive industry (lumbering), protected practice of certain professions[8], industrial transformation, transport etc. Conversely, although there have been substantial incursions into certain key areas such as business, the professions and management in some sectors through a West-East direction, these are not substantial as the bulk of immigrants is concentrated around the provision of largely unskilled or semi-skilled labour in industry and agriculture, petty trade or self-employment. Even involvement in business is undermined by ethnic monopolies of specific sectors of the economy (cf. Warnier 1994) and the sheer weight of transnational capital which leaves the remaining space of capitalist involvement (which I choose to call residual capitalism) in the hands of certain ethnic interests (Bamileke and Fulbe). Whenever business thrives it is in a community apart and seems to address only the specific Anglophone community (this is the case of the striking case of the Anglophone financial markets – the credit unions, financial cooperatives and small banks such as NFC, Amity, SLC) and

---

[8] [1] For a long time most sheriff –bailiffs in English-speaking Cameroon and until recently were of French-speaking extraction.

according to the logic and imperatives of ethno-regional autonomy. When it comes to labour, recruitment is hampered by the same type of ethnic monopolies whether in the public or private sector and the nature of training which very often does not have practical application (see chapter on harmonization strategies). The only recourse is to the development of the informal sector (petty trade, crafts).

These are general trends that need to be investigated in detail. A word of caution has to be added: these trends are largely or even unplanned but are the logical consequences of other developments (such as the advent of the unitary state) which did not envisage them. They are also the factors and conditions of other more general phenomena such as the plural linguistic order we will observe in the second chapter. Furthermore, these phenomena operate at less global and thus less perceptible levels than the macro-level, a fact that explains their virtual lack of visibility to both politicians and politically-minded intellectuals whose obsession is only with denouncing taken for criticism. The trends which we have outlined here need detailed analysis which a small introductory volume of this sort does not have the ambition to describe in detail. They are so gigantic and varied that only a multidisciplinary approach will be capable of doing justice to it.

Peculiar Circumstances of Imbalances

If one were to attempt an explanation to these unequal exchanges one would have to look at the peculiarities or specific characteristics of the migrating communities at the end of the colonial period, the experiences within the federal experiment and the conditions in which the advent of the unitary state came into being. At the close of the colonial period and the beginning of the post-independence period, the two territories that would form the federal experiment had substantial imbalances not only in demographic weight but also in human capital formation. The newly independent French-speaking of Cameroon inherited an education system characterized by a proportionately large number of public primary and post-primary institutions, an equally significant number of schools (primary, post-primary) run by missionary bodies and a tradition of scholarship to study in the colonial metropolis. Diversified as the training was, this accounted for an eventual proportionate edge within the union experience especially when this tradition was intensified deep into independence. Conversely, the Southern Cameroon's situation was characterized by a few primary schools (run by the colonial administration, Native Authority administration and the Christian missions) and only two secondary schools run by the Roman Catholic and Protestant Basel missions. The only outlet was studying in Nigeria and even then while there were a sizable number of graduates of French-speaking origins at independence, one could boast of a few in English-speaking Cameroonians of the same level. Moreover, the diversification of French-speaking education (to include technical and commercial education) as opposed to a tradition of dominantly grammar education – differences that have survived largely till this day – accounts for some of these differentials. These imbalances that later on reflected themselves in the university orientation of students of the different communities only worsened the trends at the level of technical skills and competences.

The federal experience, while allowing the French-speaking community to continue its colonial heritage – in the spirit of separate spheres of political influence agreed upon by its main architects (Foncha, Ahidjo) –, enabled the English community to institute its own schools in the now so-called "Anglo-Saxon" tradition (which was but a replication of the model that obtained in the grammar schools run by Christian missionaries or the colonial government in Nigeria). Throughout this period only one technical school was opened and state-run at Ombe. With other private initiatives, these schools trained in an English-speaking tradition and prepared its students for certificates offered by organisations based in Britain (in this case the examinations run by the Universities of Cambridge and London Examinations Boards). Alongside these school, other initiatives of the West Cameroon federated state tended to create its own insular job market (however limited) either by the institution of public economic concerns (banks, development agencies, the management of concerns left by the colonial administration, produce marketing organizations) or the provision of encouragement incentives to a budding business community. In relation to the latter one can observe the emergence of a crop of businessmen whose success became household names for quite a long time (Nangah, Che, Niba, Kilo, etc.).

These experiences created a situation of relative autonomy for a region that had come out of a colonial experience with bitter memories of a form of abject indirect rule through the regional elite of another territory. Notwithstanding the abuses of the governing class of this period and its internecine disputes, which account for the personal failures of those concerned, this experience remains one projected as the Golden Age of the

English-speaking Cameroonian and is fondly remembered for its positive aspects by those who lived it (to the extent that it is confused with Southern Cameroons). One may need to study the characteristics of employment and labour as well as the evolution of business during this period to understand the importance of the assertions made here. Unfortunately most studies pay disproportionate attention either to the abuses of officials (which were real anyway) or the profiteering of Ahidjo and his friends in the context (Ngoh et al 2004, Konings and Nyamnjoh 2003). In the meantime, the French-speaking Cameroon business situation had evolved into one dominated either by foreign business concerns – mainly European (French, Italian, Greek, Lebanese, British) – or the ethnic monopolies of the Fulbé (propped up by Ahidjo) and the so-called Bamileke (alienated from politics by the repression of the post-independence period to occupy the space of residual capitalism).

The disarticulating effect of the unitary state has been amply reported (Ngoh et al. op. cit.; Konings and Nyamnjoh 2003). Suffice it to say here that the dismantling of some of the economic institutions of West Cameroon or their abrupt immersion into a totally different business world had far-reaching consequences on the equation of human capital formation and deployment than has been reported. The demise of some of these institutions after "nationalisation" (Cameroon Bank, PMO to become NPMB) due to evident abuses is the saddest thing to have happened. Dismantling this emerging economic framework meant a brutal obligation of the business market and labour to merge and float freely in a single market where forces were not equal. The politicians who orchestrated these processes were oblivious of the fact that all policies with uniform applicability irrespective of differences or inequality invariably disfavour only the weak. That is what precisely obtained after the advent of political centralisation and the decreeing of an immutable "one and indivisible" Cameroon. How far this has fared still needs to be studied in detail.

Political and Administrative Culture: A Peculiar Monster

The dynamic of the transition into independence or "the way sovereignty was transferred" accounts as much for Africa's continuing subjection/subaltern portion within the global interstate system especially neocolonialism for a long time after independence, marginalization within the present system dated by neo-liberalism (that goes under the name of globalization) as for the failure of leadership on its own. If the allegiance of the leaders the former colonial powers was the work of legal trappings (treaties) that maintained the nominally independent countries to the former colonial powers, the "factionalisation" of leadership weakened the internal dynamics that could have provided the impetus for a viable, unified independence project. The resulted factionalisation was direct through a division between those willing to play according to the rules of the game – the "interlocuteurs valables" of the French or Fanon's "spoilt children of colonialism" or "enfants gatés"– who were to be handed over power, on the one hand, and the radicals who were excluded by all means. In the latter regard, the advocates of radical nationalism where excluded legally when their movement were outlawed as in the case of the UPC, politically when they were demonized as violent, pro-Nazi or pro-communist (depending on the ideological and political climate) and in military terms when they were countered by the force of arms and either eliminated physically or sent underground, the eventual outcome being capitulation or a protracted civil way (as in the cases of the UPC). In some cases, the radicals were forced to change camp or soften in order to be accepted as in the case of the RDA (Benot op. cit.: 146-157).

One often forgotten dimension of this fractionalization was the institution of a competitive logic among the "leadership" whose final outcome would be an internal bickering within the new leadership which in the 1960s would lead to three of Africa's critical political problems with far reaching consequences: civil wars, the temptation to resort to the use of arms in the quest for power leading to the suspension of democracy, and ethnic divisions. This competitive logic had both formal and informal aspects. The formal dimension was the call for local leadership to form political parties with no real political education and with no progammes. This led in all cases to the multiplication of political formation for the sake of it and eventually to a resort to a tribal language in the search for an electoral base. It is at this juncture that one has to situate the mistaken belief that multipartyism cannot properly function in Africa because it will be given an ethnic colour and that ethnic realities are inimical and antithetical to pluralistic politics. In fact, in the case of French Cameroons the "politicians" were even encouraged to operate within this ethnic frame, within the dominant structure of Aujoulat's BDC as the logic of politically correct competition limited the actors to their regions (Ahidjo to the North, Mbida to the Centre, South and East, Djoumessi to the Bamileke region; Soppo Priso to the Littoral). Everything was done to contain the nationalist drive of the UPC and confine it to the Bamileke and Bassa country. Even within this formal partisan frame the colonial powers had their preferences and this explains the distortions in the electoral processes within the decolonization process as well as the exclusion of many a radical political party or repression during decolonization. One can say that this pseudo-multipartyism was one of the selection techniques of the colonial regimes in order to ensure the transfer of power in the way it wanted it to be.

A corollary of this trend was the system of petty advantages/privileges that colonial administrators used in making distinction within the native communities. This is the system that generated its petty officials (clerks, teachers, the "fonctionnaires indigènes" of the French system) to which were open certain privileges (steady salaries, chiefs and allowances) and some favours as associates (albeit as subalterns) within the colonial system. It is this small segment or class that competed within itself within the dying days of colonialism for nomination and representation within the representative structures that went for self-rule or internal government. The rancour that this generated has lasted far beyond this small period. Winning itself became a goal because it opened up the subalterns to privilege and nothing else. It is in this way that bitter rivalries soon erupted between aspirants to appointment or representative office. In the same way, when one of the political actors took a certain ideological stance the other was obliged to take the opposite for the simple sake of doing so. Not before long difference took on a personalized twist. Moreover, politics developed into a game of outsmarting others. When the issue of independence was on the agenda it was perceived by the actors within the same perspective but as a struggle for a supreme monopoly mechanism where the winner will take it all from colonists against radicals all this dictated by the dynamics of privilege. Sovereignty for the winner would mean final control of ultimate authority, power and privilege. This is the origin of the self-centered vision of a leadership that is bereft of programme and ideas. This, much more than ethnic affinity, or essential primordialism, explains the bitter conflicts that have paralyzed politics ever since.

The institution of the one-party state was the official subterfuge or alibi by the "successful politicians" who would wish to keep monopoly. Conflicts (violent for the most part) were the consequences of the inability of the ruling segment to arrive at consensual arrangements. A near-Hobbesian theory of ethnicity as the war-of-all- against-all was the intellectual corollary of this development. Nyamnjoh's description of this as a "[unity] by ethnic ambition" is the expression of the illusion that this situation could be solved by a formula that would make for an ethnic allocation of resources. Such a formula has failed finally because the dynamics of privilege and division seems to be over-riding above all else and because the criteria for this ethnic allocation is rather difficult to determine. Moreover, ethnicity has come to be redefined in colonial terms to mean ethno-regionalism and organized arbitrarily to reflect artificial blocks carved out along colonial lines. This is even reinterpreted by the elites of dominant people within the region of mean privilege for themselves. Some intellectuals have also come to agree with the salience of this reasoning which gives the impression of an absence of alternatives or "fields of possibles" (Bourdieu).

The struggle for a monopoly leads to a situation where the winner in a winner-take-all logic can only achieve hegemonic consensus by building a tribal power base within his own ethnic group and then proceeding to co-opt willing collaborators from the other groups reduced to a status similar to that of natives in the colonial state. Indeed their own version of national unity is a replay of "indirect rule" wherein rulership or government is reduced to a ritual where lip-service is paid to the essential functions while the concentration is on the access to privilege. It is in this regard that the states' resources are treated as booty by the dominant ethnic entity that has achieved power (Fulbe and then Beti). Then sets in a rather unequal allocation of state resource in an illicit, illegal and illegitimate style in which process family and friendship ties, ethnic networks and cooptation are major driving forces. The most strategic positions which are priority areas go to friends and family and then by extension the tribe as arbitrarily reconstituted or redefined to mean regional group. The major instrument of state control especially the repressive apparatus are controlled by the ethnic nucleus. Care is also made to ensure that this category also has a lion share in an unbalanced so-called regional balance arrangement. The co-opted members of government are an insignificant minority who are made to perceive their status as a privilege to the one who won it all and has become a re-distributor of privileges. There are some attempts to redirect resources as a priority to the areas of the dominant group but this is only a smokescreen since the concern is not meant to improve general social conditions. The driving force is individual privileges.

When the "tribal area" is invited to participate, it is summoned a spirit of hate to provide the activists, the militia, and the bulk of the repressive apparatus. For example, the two successive regimes have recruited army, police, gendarmerie and all sorts of armed forces principally from their ethnic circles. This explains why police and army of this nature will behave out of their tribal areas as occupation forces or colonial native soldiers in foreigner captured territory because it is required to serve the interest of a deified person or persons. Within the under-privileged group the struggle for the few privileged positions remaining is so fierce that it is a destabilizing force.

The talk of regional balance is either a smokescreen (as in the Ahidjo regime) or it is just purely abandoned when it will become a stumbling block to a hardly veiled hegemony/domination by some elites of the dominant ethnic group. It is even clearly argued against as being contrary to the principle of equity in competition or abandoned in favour of some distorted universally adopted social policy strategies (e.g. the case of autochthony discourse with the invention of the concept of indigenous minorities). In any case, regional balance is an empty slogan when it does not have a consensus formula or is not operationalized.

The history of this mode of socio-political life is essentially characterized by a lavish life style, what one can call a permanent feast by the happy few in a state whose presence shines is felt only as the locus of privilege (beautiful houses, sumptuous banquets, access to easy life, the outstanding personalities by virtue of their physical appearance, etc.). This state can rightly be called a feasting state and the metaphor is the cake. It attracts by its promise to provide a portion to those who can get to the table. However, it is also one that divides by excluding rivals and the majority. The metaphor of the cake is luring but also misleading. It is not a cake to be produced but only one that appears from no where to be shared. It is not a cake shared communally but the object of rapacious competition.

The luring attractiveness of this metaphor is clearly manifest to tribal people. They will have access though self-appointed representatives, "their sons in high places" if these sons were given the chance. In fact, the reasoning is that these sons are not represented as they ought to be. By extension because the sons of other tribes are in high places, their own sons must be there. More still, since the sons of the other tribes are in high places and control resources, we should be given the chance for our sons to be there and do same. This is beautifully summed up in the following formula by Kauzya:

Every ethnic group wishes to see its sons and daughters employed so that they bring something back home. No ethnic group wishes to be absent at the national dining table where the national cake is shared. Employment in the public service is a source of pride for those whom ethnicity is a highly sentimental affair. Positions in the public service are seen as symbols of ethnic power and superiority or at least equality to other ethnic groups [...]. Ethnic groups have a belief [...] that if they are not represented in the process of public policy-making, they will lose out in the services they receive and development opportunities, programmes and projects coming to them [...] (Kauzya 2001: 113).

Reasoning by figures of speech may be dangerously spurious from a scientific standpoint. For instance, the thing that is compares in a metaphor may not be equal in reality even if there may be some basis for comparison. State resources are not "a cake" and "state personnel" will not be bound by filial ethics of allegiance to the family. Even then, ethnic groups are not families and, as such, will not have such expectations of members. State, family and ethnic group logics are essentially different. The confusion in categories is meant to convene an unsuspecting public to a false debate. It is an argument in the absence of a plausible argument. It subtracts from the universal and transcendental character of the state and sidetracks the question of difference and diversity which has its own specific character. It leaves the state in an ambivalent and stalled position compounded by the lethargy instilled through the culture of permanent feasting; this state becomes a failed state in the reality of it.

Each outing (sports event, ministerial visit, presidential tour) is an overt show of splendor and glamour as well as a display of lavish expenditure. This is the dynamics of the feasting state which cohabits with repression on those who dare protest or hold contrary views. It also cohabits with squalor and misery that it ignores because those in control do not fill responsible for what is wrong. Poor people are said to be poor because they are poor and are considered the unsuccessful. In fact, success is measured by one's proximity to power and state control. Other form of success are minimized, trivialized or made subject to the bureaucratic power structure. If one is not in administrative one is not in control. This is the ridiculous fate of the business class and intellectuals who "must" find legitimacy only in some office within the bureaucratic and other instances of the state. Witness the trend among business men and intellectual who must have a place within the state either by appointment or through election (into parliament, local councils) despite their evident success in their own spheres).

Politics then gradually became a game of intrigues in the positioning of individuals within the state apparatus. Ideological programming has been absent; talk less of programmes worth the name. Attempts at defining alternatives have always been severely met with naked repression and their champions driven underground or eliminated form the competitive politics that characterized the decolonization phase. This type of politics itself was an empty exercise that pitted the actors against each other. In the absence of real, founded arguments the competition concentrated the energies of the actors in a game of winning–for–winning sake. In this vacuum even the substance of decolonization itself, nationalism, was emptied of its content. It was an orientation towards replacement of the colonial administrators by locals and not a reformulation of the basis of the autonomous statehood and accompanying sense of peoplehood to which actors should have aspired to. In the absence of real issues, debates were trivialized and diverted towards non-essential issues such as interpersonal squabbles or inter-ethnic and inter-religious animosities.

One outcome of this competitive mode of decolonization politics that is hardly underlined and treated with an unsuspecting naivety is that it was essentially polarizing all over the world. Factionalising resulted in bickering and in absence of arguments resulted in the resort to tribal arguments and mobilizing around those lines. Such divisions essentially resulted in the weakening of champions of independence as it also kept the agenda of decolonization in the hands of the colonial power. This explains why decolonization could be conducted in the absence of negotiating as a measure within enlightened colonialism (Van Niewenhuijze) and as a prelude to continuing relations of a neo-colonial type ("special relations", "historic ties"). Without such developments resulting in the way sovereignty was transferred – which implies alternatives such as radical autonomy not around the problematic concept of nationality but around new societal projects – the nation of Cameroon should not have had its current character. The emptiness of the current mode of independence without real autonomy has its partial roots in this decolonization phase. It is important to note that this is not only true of Cameroon but was a generalized phenomenon in French and English speaking Africa. One effect was the postponement of political radicalism till later, its transfer to the amphitheatres (where it had to a limited hearing and was of no effect) and its resurfacing only later on in the 1990s.

Public policy is totally ignored or never articulated at all, preoccupied as this group is with the glamour that the state provides. On the contrary, high sounding and deceptive slogans are crafted and repeated endlessly to the extent that they are an end in themselves. Take the talk of national unity or national integration that has been the sing-song of the two regimes: in reality, they have become pure empty talk with no implementation. The emptiness of such sloganeering is concealed in grandiloquent and luring speeches such as the ones of the Ahidjo era or articulate campaigns with no innovative content as with the Biya regime. The discourses are replete with meaningless oxymoron ("libéralisme planifié"; "libéralisme communautaire")[9] or a replay of international fads with no commitment on the part of the leadership. It is either a play to the gallery or speeches meant to cajole the international community. The preoccupation with splendor ends up rendering the thinking capacity of this group numb. They are simply incapable of any innovative thinking. In the case of the Biya regime the responsibility is transferred to the international community where complete sets of slogans are lifted and parodied: "poverty alleviation or reduction", "fight against poverty", "good governance".

Lastly one can notice the emergence of the state in its naked form as a monopoly of the instruments of violence and the expression of the state as the exclusive right to violence. In its deployment of violence, it has come to be perceived an alien instance or as one that exists above society (cf. Lacroix 1985: 475). This explains the difficulties in accountability and responsiveness to general interests.

International Dimension: The Cultural Status of the State

The colonial legacies and the history of the post-World War II interstate system as a system of spheres of political and economic influence (captured in other jargon as neocolonialism) within a bipolarism that dissolved with the dissolution of the experiment in collectivism (Sovietism and its variants, Maoism) has defined states in the South (ex-Third World) in terms of their colonial cultural legacies. The choice of Southern Cameroonians that went contrary to this dominant logic placed a post-1961 Cameroon in an ambiguous position: an officially bilingual and bicultural country at least

---

[9] Liberalism is essentially opposed to the planning and communitarian philosophies of politics and economic organization.

within the federation. This equally placed its leaders in an ambiguous position as to its cultural identity and involvement in international affairs which generated an ambivalence which sought to provide answers to contradictory claims on the new state. Largely a Gaullist French creation, the new regime maintained very close bilateral ties with France within whose specific sphere of influence ("pré carré") it fell. The euphemism was the "maintenance of historic relations" or "privileged ties" which translated the willingness to remain within the relations of domination and dependency between France and Cameroon. The diversification of relations to establish formal diplomatic ties with Britain was pragmatic but was not of the same nature. That is not to insinuate that the first type of relations were a model that should have been extended to other countries. At the multilateral level the option to subscribe neither to the Commonwealth or any association between France and its former colonies was a token of dissociation from open participation in movements deriving from the colonial era. This anti-neocolonial non-alignment of a peculiar type was however undercut by Cameroon's subscription to organizations that were French-inspired and bringing together former French colonies viz. the Organization Commune Africaine et Malgache (OCAM) and the Union Douanière later to become Union Douanière et Economique de l'Afrique Centrale (UDEAC) in a regionalism that tied the countries to the former colonial power. These early associations within the community of former French colonies to be later ratified with the association of Cameroon into a regular France-Africa summit and the *Francophonie* placed Cameroon as a de facto monolingual, monocultural country in the international community. The eventual diversification of diplomatic relations to other English-speaking countries such as Nigeria and the USA in the main and subscription/admission into the Commonwealth has not changed the situation substantially (especially as ambassador to these countries are essentially French-speaking). Even the token association with the Economic Community of West African States (ECOWAS) relapsed into oblivion as this was eventually forgotten.

It is not even this status but the subscription of Cameroon to uniform treaties and practices designed within the context of regional or subregional groups within this arrangement. This is largely true of the integration of Cameroon into the CEMAC (Communauté Economique et Monetaire de l'Afrique Central) which in the replay of integration into the colonial Afrique Equatoriale Française (AEF) with its continuing monetary practices, economic integration to the benefit of French interests and the tendency towards uniform cultural practices in the latter respect. Apart from the exclusive use of French as an institutional language (which has now been extended to bank notes), CEMAC is also making incursions into uniform practices in terms of education. In an agreement between university institutions of the subregional organization the understanding is that the application is according to the majority model. There is no place for specificities such as the bicultural situation of Cameroon. The institutions that have to apply generally (e.g. COBAC, CIMA) do not also take into consideration the specificity of Cameroon's history. Other uniform treaties within this framework have brought with them exclusively French-inspired international legislation on key practices: OCAM accounting procedures from OCAM, the OHADA (organization pour Harmonisation de Droit des Affairs en Afrique) a uniform commercial law originally applicable in Francophone countries (and in the process of extension to some English speaking countries) and the CIMA code insurance legislation in favour of practices in the former French colonies. Whether these international legislative instrument and practices are of French origin or not is not important. What is of importance is the imperative of a fait accompli that this places on Cameroon's bicultural situation as it serves to subvert political claims to a bicultural option. The imposition of such practices from an international dimension, which is unsuspecting to both ordinary citizens and the academia, serves to strengthen existing cultural imbalances in favour of a Francophone Cameroon culture. The other issue is that the specific character of Cameroons identity is not asserted at the international level. In negotiating and signing these treaties, the governing elites dominated for now by an ethno-regional corps with a largely French training, does not argue or negotiate for the recognition of this specific identity. Moreover, the weight of reactions at local level is never measured. When the CFA franc was modified to carry only French denominations in words the implementers of the decision never for once foresaw any objection from English-speaking users or any difficulties that could arise in use.

Conclusions

I have traced the emergence of the Cameroonian polity from its spectacular development in a peculiar combination of historical circumstances: utopian imaginary; immature competitive politicking, recuperation and opportunism, asymmetrical negotiations and inconclusive arrangements and forced political bonding. The consequences are a political situation where a tradition of co-opting representatives for Anglophones coexists with the marginalisation of a substantial segment of the population, political and social indifference and the resort to separatism. This situation is compounded by inequalities along the lines of the linguistic divide in terms of human capital formation, deployment and employment (in proportionate terms). Finally, the continuous drift of the state towards a French-speaking tradition and practices as it identifies itself predominantly with the French-speaking community at international level only goes to reinforce the forced political order which gives primacy to French and institutes a comprehensive set of imbalances (political, economic, social, cultural) in its wake.

The union experiment between the territories formerly under the United Nations mandate as administered by the British and the French in the Cameroons is often presented in a simplistic manner as the result of a plebiscite and negotiated reunification pitting principally politicians of the Southern Cameroons territory and the leaders of the independent French speaking Republic of Cameroon. What is taken for granted is the union idea that is never critically analysed. The rising opposition to this idea within Anglophone autonomist circles accompanied by increasing disenchantment from the larger segments of that population calls for a critical analysis of the conditions under which the union was crafted and ho this has developed into a problematic situation. This paper traces the genesis of the union idea to the utopian idealism contained in the firm calls by the *Union des Populations du Cameroun* (UPC) for unification and immediate independence but argues that the conditions under which this was achieved were totally different from what its initiators had imagined. The actors were not the same as the initiators and were driven by motives directly opposed to the original vision of radical nationalism.

To demonstrate this argument an attempt is made to understand the logic of the UPC struggles in the immediate post-World War II period characterised by the bipolar competition between the two major ideological blocks, the attitudes of the colonial administrations to decolonisation, the conditions that fashioned the development of competing visions of independence and the conditions under which the Cameroons territories obtained independence and eventually united. The objective is to demonstrate that although the UPC radical vision had become the dominant idea about decolonisation in the French Cameroons to the extent that it had captured the imaginary of politicians in the British Southern Cameroons, the

North of the territory under French rule had been developed into an entity apart to the extent that it openly cultivated a separatist spirit in relation to the South characterised by its progressive definition as and adoption of a conservative Muslim identity that was opposed to both the majority Kirdi (lit. non-Muslim) indigenes of that area but to radical nationalism. This as one of the factors that were to be played against the nationalists in favour of independence that would be more accommodating to continuing influence from the former colonial power, the others being the disqualification and banning of the UPC from the normal political process. The resort by the UPC to an ill-equipped and ill-prepared armed struggle that went far into independence (early 1970s) that was the excuse for a brutish repression by both colonial and post-colonial authorities only went to complicate the union process and shape political culture in a very peculiar manner. At the beginning of the union contrasting drives could be observed within the polity: utopian unionist visions of the Anglophones torn between the euphoria of the contracting politicians and frustration from others who could immediately observe reciprocation from French-speaking counterparts; a UPC torn, splintered and driven either into exile, capitulating to Ahidjo's version of *ralliement* or putting up a weak resistance for a decade; pragmatic profiteering and rising autocratic rule by the Ahidjo regime.

These contrasting drives have survived to constitute three streams of political culture which run or parallel to and occasionally counter to each other:

- Radical nationalism that is often associated with a certain utopian unionism and a profound democratic ideal. This stream has its roots both in the radical nationalism of the UPC (with its close association to wider anti-colonial movements of the 1950s and 1960s), the perceived experience of the Anglophone component under British colonial rule and a certain pan-Kamerun ideal that fosters conviviality across the Anglophone-Francophone divide;

- A culture of autocratic rule by successive regimes of the successor state. This is characterised by the following trends: a monopoly of a class of politicians over the state apparatus (which de facto excludes the possibility for a genuine democracy); a tradition of bureaucratic high-handedness that reinforces non-democratic forms of government; an unending legacy of brutish repression that resurfaces at every indication of dissent, protest and opposition whether violent or peaceful; and a tradition of ethno-regionalism that shares power unequally between regions (with the attendant drift in terms of tribalism, nepotism and a tribal monopoly of state resources and capital);

A culture of permanent discontent and, even, dissent from segments of the polity that have been victims of abuses at several critical phases of the country's history beginning with the decolonisation phase. This is expressed in ordinary conversation, street protest, academic writing, the media, artistic creation (song, literature, satire) and even the threat of armed conflict, in some cases aimed at the overthrow of government (from exile) and in some cases dissociation from the polity (secession). This is the source of what can be described as instability and uncertainty at the level of both the State and society.

Chapter Two

The Making of Ethnic Frontiers as Statecraft

One question that apparently looks simple but which is complex is that of how ethnic spaces become political spaces in the modern period or how politics in the modern period is played in the ethnic domain whereas the rules of the game indicate that it has to be played in neutral trans-ethnic spaces. A related question will be that of understanding why peoples once connected to each other suddenly become strongly divided in the terrain of modern politics. This paper attempts a global examination of these questions and their importance for both theory and practice taking Cameroon for an example. The argument it hopes to articulate is that post-colonial administrative (in the heels of colonial policy) attempts to restructure the ordering of space of the peopling has disarticulated old modes of interconnectivity and created new unworkable ethno-regional blocks that serve no other purpose than politics. This is not to repeat what others have said either in the sweeping epithets used to qualify every post-colonial situation. I wish to show how the specific historical facts of Cameroon's history have shaped its own creation of its ethnic dilemma both for the governed and the governed. I wish to demonstrate how the political decisions of territorial re-ordering shaped both the attitudes of the governing to the local peoples and how the latter responded to these processes through self-awareness that came to underline cleavages. I will combine secondary data (administrative archives, written reports, administrative texts) with first hand informant reports in my analysis which is definitely going to be historical, anthropological and sociological, the three dimensions constituting facets of the same human facts.

In the process therefore I do not only look at official policy (legislation and sloganeering) and practice; I also examine unofficial (and even officious) practices that take the real dimension of policy, the reactions of local peoples (adjustment of elite whether traditional or modern, mass mobilization) and the development of social categories of perception developed in the process. I use the term frontier in two senses but which are complementary. The first sense, which is the obvious, is that of physical delimitation of territorial scope of a unit. This meaning refers in administrative terms to where the administrative competence of an officer or a traditional authority ends. Such a definition is often oblivious of the fact that, as mental constructs that apply to human space, they are also frames of reference in the perception of space. The second definition, which derives from this conceptual clarification, therefore is specifically the mental dimension that may correspond to physical and territorial limits but which in the modern manifestations of ethnicity are essentially mental. This is the substance of what has been styled erroneously geopolitics. I hope to show how both types of constructs have been created over time. The paper is organized in three parts. The first two analyse the strategies adopted by the two regime that have governed Cameroon successively in the postcolonial period while the third discusses the dynamics at work in the creation of ethnic frontiers as it enters into a dialectical contradiction with the process of state formation.

An Outline of the Political Arithmetic of the Ahidjo Regime

Ahidjo's ultimate emergence as leader of the newly independent Republic of Cameroon was a result of the French colonial ordering of political relations as a containment of nationalism that was characteristic of the South (more literate and politically advanced) and a choice of the Fulbé as a more accommodating element as opposed both to the Southerners and the non-Muslim Northerners. This also meant that the Fulbé element had to be constructed as dominant politically in its Northern sphere where they were a demographic minority and in the whole of Cameroon where they were both obscure and backward. It was therefore incumbent on Ahidjo himself and his Northern clique of the "Bloc du Nord" to construct the myth of the dominant North as the pivotal force in a new political arithmetic where other regions would simple be associated. This process of developing the Northern Fulbé into a dominant ethno-regional block is described succinctly by most independent thinking observers of the decolonization phase (Mongo Beti 2003:81-83; 252-263; Ateba Yene 1988; Wonyu 1985). In order to achieve this hegemony Ahidjo had to resort to a three fold policy: repression and elimination of the nationalist forces of the UPC; intimidation of leaders of political parties with a base in the South leading either to their elimination from politics or their purely physical elimination (Mongo Beti ibid: 258-261; Ateba Yene ibid: 145-46; Bayart 1978: 45 - 65); institution of a *de facto* one party system with a Fulbé hegemony at its base.

Ahidjo's regime as true legacy of the colonial regime continued with the repressive policies that had targeted the UPC in the West and Sanaga-

Maritime regions as he embarked on a process of "pacification" with the assistance of French troops. Such a strategy was evidently accompanied by the political marginalization of the regions in question or the substitution of nationalist leaders with more accommodating personalities some of whom were artificially probed. By 1962 most political parties in the South were openly being intimidated to fuse into the Union Camerounaise (UC), which was but an extension of the Northern Block of the pre-independence situation and which was evolving into a *de facto* one-party state.

Things did not work out so smoothly for the Ahidjo regime, at least, as fast as could have been expected. The process of self-determination in the British mandated territories came to modify the picture considerably and slowed down the process itself for at least a decade. The process that goes by the name of plebiscite on either reunification with the newly independent French-speaking Republic of Cameroon or integration into Nigeria was driven by two forms of idealization-cum-*utopias*. These idealizations were generated by the historical conditions in which the peoples and nationalist elites were living. While Southern Cameroons nationalists were confronted with some form of proxy colonization via Ibo or Nigerian domination, which served as a deterrent to integration within Nigeria as an independence option, this making of the French sphere a potential zone of refuge, repression in the French mandated territories made of the British territories an ideal zone of refuge from the repressive inferno (Gooderidge op. cit.: 40). As such, reunification was more of a *utopia* for Anglophones in the escape from the relegation of their status of colonial subjects to the very extreme of marginality. The standard bearers of the pan-Kamerun idea, of which the UPC were the leading proponents, were driven by the idealization of the British sphere as the epitome of virtuous governance: freedoms within the colonial regime, absence of a repressive machinery etc.

This idealization was far from reality as this was but a refracted reading from a distance. The unionists of the French Cameroons were as oblivious of the integrationist intentions of the British colonial authorities as the unionists in the British Cameroons were oblivious of the neo-colonial intentions in the decolonisation arrangements of the French that did not only exclude their counterparts, the UPC, but inscribed independence within an ethno-regional perspective. It is the greatest irony of Cameroon's independence and unification that pan-Kamerun activists in the British Cameroons started off on a path that had been traced a party that would be which from power and the dynamics of decolonization.[10] I advance the argument that there was a problem of visibility in the utopia that drove the movement towards unity, the steam of the utopia sustaining the enthusiasm of the unification project right into the contemporary period and the lack of visibility and naivety of the flag bearers of the utopia ushering in the dejection and frustration that English-speaking Cameroonians were going to face. It is clear that the then Premier of French Cameroons, André Marie Mbida, was not interested in the unification option: "It was not prudent for the Southern Cameroons to be seen to be forcing itself unto an uninviting brother" (Amazee 2004: 19). It is also common knowledge that the expectations of Ahidjo and his Northern block were that the British Northern Cameroons should vote for unification with the newly independent Republic of Cameroon in order to bolster their ethno-regional hegemonic designs. Southern Cameroons was thus of little significance in his design. Such expectations were also naïve as they were oblivious of overt British intentions of integrating the British Cameroons into Nigeria. With the vote in Southern Cameroons in favour of the independent Republic of Cameroon and that of Northern Cameroons in favour of Nigeria a new factor was integrated into the emerging ethno-regional artifice, not to be confused with a pre-existing ethnic mosaic difficult to transform into a nation (Levine 1964) - that was to be the building block of an ethno-regional arithmetic.

The new arithmetic had at its centre the hegemony of a Northern Fulbé block to which were to be associated accommodating elements created to represent an artificially created Centre-South-East region in an alliance wrongly referred to as a North-South alliance. The coastal peoples were not to be excluded but placed at the periphery where they would be largely rid of any political potential. Half of the western region (what is called the Bamileke region) pacified through repression and political debauchery was to be depoliticized and bought off with economic concessions as they were cut off from the Bamum, who themselves had been artificially disconnected from the West and politically (ideologically) connected to the "Muslim" North by way of supposed religious affinities. These developments have their origins in French colonial administrative policy during the mandate period but go beyond that to the antecedents of the German colonial administration that

---

[10] Both Endeley and Foncha are reported to have had separate and consistent contacts with the UPC at different times, Endeley before the UPC was outlawed (Ngoh 1990a; Gooderidge 2004: 39) and Foncha in the immediate pre-independence days and the immediate post-independence period (Gooderidge ibid.: 30-40).

governed "northern Cameroon under special conditions" in which "Muslim rulers saw that they assumed more responsibility than before [their] conquest" (Njeuma 2002: 57), a form of Indirect Rule that involved "power sharing" (ibid.: 56). The French continued this system which was inscribed within its political geography of the mandate period that can be divided into two: a pre-World War II and a post-War II period. Prior to the War most of the territory continued in the pattern of demarcations initiated by the Germans which had stressed administrative rather then political considerations in the carving of the "circonscriptions" of 1916 (Ngoh 1990:77) and the "regions", "sub-divisions" and "posts" by the mid-1940s (Bouchaud 1944:17). The emerging Douala metropolis shared the functions of de facto capital with Yaoundé although the heart of administration was Douala itself. Colonial perceptions of the territory changed in the aftermath of the war with the development of political protest in the late 1940s. This was to start with Duala protests over the land question in the tradition of the protest of the tail end of the German protectorate and that continued into the interwar period. It is not therefore by mistake that the first radical left wing movements (trade unions, student unions) and the first nationalist political party was born in Douala and led by people of coastal origins in the main (see Derrick 1989; Austen and Derrick 1999). The Duala themselves were in an ambiguous position as they resented French colonial practices (maltreatment during the war, relegation of indigenous people to a subordinate status). Open hostility towards the French presence and preference for other imperial powers (e.g. the English, German) should not be overlooked in any analysis of the development of radical nationalism in the French mandate territory (Amazee 2003: 157).

This factor in turn fashioned the attitudes of French colonial authorities in the reconfiguration of the territory. Firstly the powers of the Duala chiefs were largely reduced and Douala reduced in political importance as an important centre of the territory. Secondly, the status of Yaoundé was enhanced and it grew into the substantive capital of Cameroon concomitant with the extension of the ethnic frontiers of the Beti Groups around Yaoundé whose new category of "chef supérieur" was given wider powers far beyond the ethnic boundaries of his own group (Ngoh ibid: 80-81). Thirdly, when the UPC emerged as a radical movement, rival ethnic-based associations and political formations were encouraged and assisted by the colonial administration in the South of the country. This was the raison d'être behind the creation of *Bloc Démocratique du Cameroun* (BDC) which was hastily crafted only as an ethno-regional patchwork between the Beti (Mbida), Duala (Soppo Priso) and the North (Ahidjo). Initially the French choice of an accommodating leadership was that of the Beti represented by Mbida considered as "interlocuteur valable" (Awasom and Ettangondop 2001: 67) until the latter turned out to be unpredictable. Moreover the representation of French Cameroons into the Legislative Assembly of French Cameroons in 1957 reflected a geo-ethnic arrangement where the North and Bamum had a majority of 30 as against 20 for the Centre and South, 9 for the Bamileke, 8 for the Littoral and 3 independent candidates (Awasom and Ettangondop ibid.: 65). When this strategy did not yield the desired result of containing the rising tide of the nationalist demands of the UPC, the "north" with its rather scanty Muslim population was carved out and bolstered as a Muslim enclave through an ideology of Islamic difference. This was the more so as even the apparently accommodating Beti elite were becoming more and more unpredictable as many of their elites either joined the UPC or echoed their nationalist demands. Dongmo describes this reconfiguration of the ethnic situation in the following terms:

> ...the unification of North Cameroon as a region was from the beginning an initiative of the colonial power in its search for an alibi to justify its continued presence vis-à-vis claims for independence before this was appropriated by elites of this region in their own interests. Archives show that the colonial power invented a "muslim problem", by presenting a Muslim North Cameroon that had to be managed differently from a Christian South Cameroon, a traditional and poor North that had to be protected against the risk of domination by a modernised and almost developed South. (Dongmo 1997: 276; *translation mine*)

French cultivated Fulbé separatism was even exploited by the traditional elite to use to argue for secession in case independence turned out to be unfavourable to their interests vis-à-vis a "more developed" southern part of the country (Dongmo ibid.: 267). It is significant to note that a similar attitude was adopted by elites of the Northern Hausa-Fulani complex in neighbouring Nigeria with the blessing of the British colonial authorities.

The policy of Islamic difference had two extra dimensions that were internal to the North and the Western regions. In the North the conservative Muslim elites were pitted against the more backward non-Muslim so-called

"Kirdi"[1], with this policy becoming heightened as some of the non-Muslim peoples such as the Baya were openly rebellious (Ngoh 1990, Burnham 1996). French colonial reports had always treated these peoples as resistant to both Fulbé domination and, later on, French colonialism. It is therefore clear that Fulbé domination of the Northern region was achieved with the assistance of the colonial administration partly by recognising and codifying this dominant position and partly by using the Fulbé aristocracy as official representatives in a policy of Indirect Rule that did not officially declare itself but, which we have seen, was a simple continuation of a strategy initiated by the Germans. This affirmation is bolstered by Mongo Beti's assertion that the persistence of marginal peoples right into the postcolonial period and especially the indomitable "Kirdi" was proof of the fact that Fulbé domination was hardly complete before the advent of the colonial project (Mongo Beti 2003: 81).

In the western region the policy was to segregate the Bamum from the Bamileke on both grounds of religions difference and political ideology. The so-called Muslim Bamum were thus constituted into a bastion of support to the colonial administration as the Bamileke had become openly anti-colonial supporters of the UPC (Mouiche 1997). Dongmo goes further to indicate that French colonial authorities also invented the Bamileke question in order to exclude them from the power as he argues that ethnicity was a key factor in the demarcation of administrative units and the invention of new terminology such as the "département Bamileke" and département Bamoun" (Dongmo ibid: 312). Mouiche (op. cit.) has also demonstrated how such divisions in the Western region, where the Bamum and its neighbours (carved out into separate ethno-regional entities) had a variety of social ties, was manipulated in the policy of containment of nationalist demands or support for colonial authority as early as the late 1940s. As such, we have, on the one hand, a macro-regional division between a North made up of Muslim elements and a South with a Christianising and modernizing future and, on the other, micro-regional divisions at a more localized level invented to both enlist support for colonial interests and contain rising nationalist demands. Such divisions were not only instrumental in the decolonisation process; they served as part of the new politics of neo-colonial containment and an internal political arithmetic.

---

[1] Non Fulbé Northerners.

The response to nationalist demands with ethnic balkanisation, manipulation and containment reflected itself in the decolonisation process. In both the French mandated territory and the Southern Cameroons the independence questions shifted from the national terrain in the years running from the late 1940s to the verge of independence in the early 1960s. North-South cleavages were manipulated in both spheres of the mandate to secure the ascendance to power of "Northern elements", in one case, the natives of the "Grassfields" (led by Foncha) and, in another, the Northern Fulbé Muslim block. However, this was the farthest such a policy could achieve.

As every other political formation in Southern Cameroons flirted with the greater Kamerun idea, which was at the basis of re-unification, and brandished Ibo or Nigerian domination as an excuse for shunning integration into Nigeria, the North-South cleavage became redundant for British colonial policy. In the same vein nationalist questions were also obscured by both the ethnically motivated separation from Nigeria and internal divisions that were more in line with a politics for politics sake, the "politics of winning" or as the French put it, "la politique politicienne" where the game of ethnic numbers was crucial. In any case independence was played and won within the parameters of ethnic relations developed within the mandate period (Amazee 2004). Subsequent political developments were to move along the same lines.

In the French sphere the game was interrupted by the resort to armed struggle by the UPC as a reaction to the disbanding of the party within the logic of containment. The repression that ensued and that went right into the first decade of independence further served to both alienate the Bamileke and Bassa (plus associated) as ethnically restive entities and excluded them from the game of normal politics. In this regard one could observe a division between collaborator groups and hostile entities. The North was firmly constituted as a bastion of support for the colonial regime and its neo-colonial successor state. It is in this way that the "North" considered backward was handed over power and the South contained by a combination of repression and enticement to collaboration. This situation survived far into the Ahidjo regime, which worked on and perfected it.

In this regard, the French-speaking sphere was going to evolve along the ethno-regional lines traced by the colonial regime through a combination of force, political debauchery and terror while the former British Cameroons came to be grafted to this patchwork in a warped arrangement that went under the name of federalism. Although claiming equal status to the French

speaking section in legal, linguistic and cultural dimensions it evolved only within the framework of the ethno-regional arrangements that had been emerging and were fostered by the regime. One can opine that Ahidjo's acceptance of the federal options was just a tactical ploy both to placate the Anglophones and a way to legally cut them off from the rest of the South which continued to radically oppose the regime even up to a decade after independence. Konings and Nyamnjoh (2003: 12 - 13) report that the results of the plebiscite were a veritable shock to Ahidjo because of the very prospects the Southern Cameroons politicians coming into an alliance with fellow southern politicians in the French sphere. They show that one way of containing such a prospect was by restricting each contracting party to limit each party's activities to its initial sphere: KNDP to West Cameroon and UC to French Cameroons.

The regime also paid lip-service to the federal arrangement as the latter was subjected to the highly centralized form of the state under Fulbé hegemony. This lasted as long as the "pacification" of the South lasted and gave way for an overt centralized form of the state where the ethno-regional arrangement was more salient. The regime's strategies within the federalist arrangement undercut the pretensions of English speaking elements to equal status within the federation. When West Cameroon was classified as one of the six regions of the Federal Republic by Decree No 61-DF-15 of 20 December 1961 (that is too early into the federalist arrangement), the implication was that it was only equal to one of the regions of a vast Cameroon. The conflicts that arose out of the conflicting powers of officials of the overlapping structures (namely the regions and federated state) led to a devaluation of the status of the federated state of West Cameroon. In a combination of the Federal constitution and the unwritten tenets of the ethno-regional arrangement the president of northerner origins was to be assisted by a Vice President from West Cameroon in a presidential system where the latter was largely rid of any real powers. The rest of the regions were to be represented by hand-picked ministers who owed total allegiance to the President. The same was true of deputies to the Assembly who were tagged to regions but were actually cronies of the President. In the political arithmetic of the regime a constant balance was struck between the Northern region which remained a unified territorial entity, on the one hand, and the centre-south of the Beti-Fang-Bulu group, on the other, in terms of ministerial representation in government with the two grand regions attaining near-parity in terms of numbers (Ngayap 1983:68-87). The other regions were more or less adjuncts in the structure or simply sidelined. Ngayap's analysis (ibid) cited above hints at this but does not declare it: the Littoral area was simply marginalized while the East was clearly forgotten in the arrangement as politically irrelevant. The army and the parliament were also crafted to reflect this hegemony of the North and the marginal association of the South both in numbers and leadership. Moreover the sheer numbers of a northern dominated army and its brutality was used in warding off any opposition to the system and maintaining it.

The schemed institution of the unitary state, which legalized the hitherto disguised centrist policies which had been undercutting the federal smokescreen, meant the full integration of erstwhile of English speaking Cameroon into the ethno-regional arithmetic that had been developing during the French colonial period. If the region was a people with a claim to a different political arrangement based on constitutional guarantees which kept them apart, the 1972 constitution transformed them into an ordinary ethno-regional political block which was to be integrated into the ethno-regional patchwork that was the bedrock of Cameroon's politics as laid down in an unwritten constitution and statecraft. It is from this period that Anglophones became a "tribe" in the same sense as the other big "tribes" (Northerner, Bamileke, Beti, Bassa) that could be found in the political arithmetic of Ahidjo. It is also at this period that English speaking Cameroonians came to be increasingly perceived by ordinary Cameroonians as a tribe rather than as a component that had been associated through a contracting process. Cosmetic and token measures such as the naming of the country as "United Republic" (an obvious borrowing from other African examples such as Tanzania but with nothing in common) were simply meant to allay the fears of Anglophone autonomists who had started to be restive as the federalist arrangement started failing. In reality the informed arrangements of the ethno-regional logic prevailed as the largely ceremonial position of house speaker went to Anglophones with a dormant Prime Ministerial position going to the Beti.

What stood out clearly was the grand division between a fictitiously homogenous North (in the image of the "Bloc du Nord") and a splintered south in an arrangement where the Fulbé stood out as dominant. Biyiti Bi Essam (1984: 58) in this regard presents this situation so succinctly in the following words:

The administrative map, as Ahidjo drew it, portrays, on the one hand a single province to the North, that is the Northern Province, and, on the other, six provinces to the south. The surface area of the Northern Province is only slightly less than that of the six other provinces put together. The population census of 1976 put its population size at 2000000 or a third of the population of Cameroon at this time.

This partition is the product of a special way of perceiving Cameroon; for Ahidjo there are two entities known as Cameroon: North Cameroon and the others. Ahidjo wants that this North Cameroon be monolithic, hence this aberration of a partitioning... (*Translation mine*)

This point is given saliency by the observation that Ahidjo "drew his political support from the north acting as a block. Naturally he supported and designed policies that treated the northern region as a block, one and indivisible... Politicisation of northern Cameroon's identity was in evidence" and "used as an essential ingredient to match or ward off Southern Cameroon domination on a national scale" (Njeuma op. cit.: 62). This dichotomy was also accompanied in practice by a disconnection of the two regions as there were no attempts to create regular means of communication between them. In the partitioning of administrative units that accompanied the unitary state, the logic of ethnic exclusion played a dominant role. It has to be noted that the zoning into provinces institutionalised the regional model that had undercut or had been overlapping with the federal structure. In all, the partitioning was hegemonic and meant to ensure allegiance to the regime. The division of Anglophone Cameroon into two provinces corresponded to the Bamenda vs. Cameroons provinces division of the late 1940s, this division being largely meant to forestall the Anglophone acting as a single block in the direction of secession in the same way as Biafra although the Northern Fulbe jealously clung to the myth of their unity. Many facts point to a sustained policy of disarticulation which favoured elites as against regional development and general welfare. Firstly, there was a devaluation of the capital of the former federated state to that of a provincial capital at the same time as the development of rival centres (Bamenda, Kumba) and exclusion of areas that had voted against the unification option (Wum, Nkambe). Secondly, there was an intensification of the divide born of the KNDP government's balance sheet of exclusionary politics. For example, former KNDP elements continued to monopolise key positions attributed to Anglophones in the ethno-regional arrangement. Thirdly, the Anglophone region was disconnected by a sheer neglect of intra-regional communication networks (Mamfe-Kumba; Bamenda–Mamfe) as the new administrative units (provinces) were connected more to the new provinces in the French sphere

(Littoral, West Province), a fact which has continued to be the source of suspicion from autonomists who consider this an attempt to simply merge English speaking provinces into the Francophone sphere.[11]

The so-called policy of regional equilibrium in administration and development was often a smokescreen behind the political arithmetic of trade-offs in a situation of imbalance. In practice one could notice that the persistence of the nationalist critique as well as a growing discontent expressed in a governance-centred critique resulted in a dichotomy between pro-regime and anti-regime elites within the same regions this corroding the mirage of regional unity and representation. Secondly, there were regions tagged as pro-regime and anti-regime a fact which destroyed the myth of regional balance based on artificially designated regions. For example, when certain logics of affirmative action favoured the Anglophone and Northerners as lagging behind in modern schooling or the Bamileke in a trade-off to exclude them from politics, this only resulted in discontent in areas where alleged favours were not accorded. According to Biyiti Bi Essam (op. cit.: 87), an apologist of the 'Beti'-dominated regime of President at its early days, this meant slowing down those regions considered to be advanced and pushing ahead others considered backward. What went in the name of balance, whether administrative or developmental, was symbolic or token. There was a general appearance of all regions participating in government but this was in fact an arrangement where a few hand picked politicians stood for regions. Intra-regional conflicts between elites competing for recognition by the regime or intra-regional hegemonies (such as that of the Fulbé in the North) are glaring contradictions within the scheme.

What emerges from this analysis is that, there was no balanced development, no participation in government and no balanced government. The ten years between the institution of the unitary state in 1972 and the resignation of Ahidjo in 1982 (which did not mean an end to the regime) were characterized by fear of repression, an artificial prosperity induced by the oil boom, a generally restive or potentially boiling sports of protest (repeated university student unrest, rising Anglophone opposition to their new status albeit in an underground manner), a radical critique from exiled elites who were constantly harassed by security agents operating within a Cold War context of open repression, internal elites estranged by the

---

[11] This is bolstered by the fact that certain services (the central bank's regional offices, headquarters of military command region) meant for the North West or South West Provinces are situated in the Francophone provinces.

arrangements of the unitary state, fragile though long serving governments, stagnation of social development indicators, neglect of the greater hinterland as development policy was concentrated around a few growing metropolitan areas (Douala, Yaoundé, Garoua) (Yenshu 1997: 135), and the development of a heightened sense of regional and "tribal" consciousness paradoxically as the chief architect of the system never missed any opportunity to castigate "tribalism, nepotism, regionalism and clanism "[12].

The succession crisis of the 1982 – 1984 periods exposed the fragility of the logic of the Ahidjo regime's ethno-regional politics in the most blatant manner. As a prolongation of this logic the arrangements that went with the succession process were at the basis of the conflicts that ensued but also reflected the outcome of the conflict and the solutions that the Biya regime provided to the conflict.

Biya's Statecraft: Mirror Image and Heir

Ahidjo suddenly resigned and transferred power to Biya in less than a week at the end of 1982 in an arrangement which left the ethno-regional formula apparently intact. In the government that ensued, the element of Fulbé hegemony was maintained as the Prime Minister and several key ministries remained with the Fulbé hegemony in the North. In fact what appeared in the structure of the government was a nominal president who was not only hemmed in by Northerner Fulbé elites but one who was going to be under the beg and call of an ex-president who had kept the doctrinaire position of head of one-party structure in-charge of ideological orientation, an arrangement reminiscent of what was to emerge in the latter day Islamic republic of Iran. A series of events were to lead to confrontations with serious consequences for the logic of the ethno-regional arrangement[13]. The first is the confrontation between the new head of state and the former president. The ideological clarifications on matters of precedence laid to rest the question of protocol at the helm of the state but that laid the stage for further confrontation. The second was the threatened resignation of ministers of a Northern block alongside others from the "Muslim" enclaves of the Noun and Mbam Divisions. The response was a government shake-up that slightly modified the balance against the Fulbé elements by introducing a

---

[12] See in this regard Kegne Pokam (1986).
[13] For a comprehensive account see also Biyiti bi Essam (op. cit.). The interpretation of the events would obviously differ.

"Kirdi" interim Prime Minister and a few more Kirdi ministers while dropping key Fulbe barons. The third event was the alleged attempted assassination of President Biya by two of Ahidjo's aide-de-camps all of Northerner Fulbé origins. The trials that followed settled the matter from a judicial perspective through court martial that saw the sentencing to death of Ahidjo *in abstentia* and the conviction and execution of the alleged agents. The stage was now set for the last act that led to the bloody confrontation of April 6 1984 which saw gendarmerie elements, largely of Northerner origins and led essentially by Northerner officers, attempting to take over power in order to maintain the status quo. The coup attempt was rapidly crushed with the army and court martial settled the judicial side of the question.

Parallel to these rather spontaneous tactical responses to the events, Biya and his regime also reacted with ethno-regional strategies that have since marked his own political formula. The first of the acts of reordering of institutional arrangements of the previous regime was reducing the weight of the Fulbé in the ethno-regional arrangements in a two- way process. One strategy was fractioning the North (with its claim to a hegemonic block) into three provinces of near equal size and demographic weight. This was accompanied by a process in which the status of the Kirdi was enhanced with appointments into some key positions as against less Fulbé and where the hegemony of the Fulbé of Garoua was devalued by the promotion of elites from the new provincial centres of Maroua and Ngaoundere. A second strategy was the adjustment of the ethno-regional formula at global level by replacing the Fulbé with the "Kirdi" as representatives of the North. As such, Ayang Luc, Christian of "Kirdi" origins, became interim Prime Minister in lieu of Bello Bouba Maigari. Since then other kirdi or non-Fulbé elements have continued to hold key positions as a counterweight to Fulbé hegemony. "This was the greatest blow to Islamo-Fulbé hegemony, which had significantly propelled and sustained [a] regional identity, begun nearly two centuries back in history" (Njeuma op. cit.: 64). Anglophones were left to their largely ceremonial role at the summit of the state[14].

The second major set of measures that the Biya regime took was a dismantling the political arithmetic based on concessions towards certain restive segments such as Anglophones and the Bamileke. The constitutional revision which deleted the token term "United" from the designation of the

---

[14] The position of Speaker of House, Chancellor of National Orders and Premier, attributed to Anglophones go with largely reduced powers.

state and the replacement of the slogan of *unity* which had been at the base of Ahidjo's "Anglophone policy" (meant to faintly remind them of a separate history and identity within the polity) with that of *integration* was inscribed within this strategy. Beyond the symbolic level the argument was that all Cameroonians were to be treated at the same level in all domains because they were equal and that no special affirmative action type concessions were to be accorded any groups of people anymore; hence Biya's adamant refusal to come back on the principal characteristics of this reform. The argument of architects of the regime is that the concessions had led to privilege for some ethno-regional blocks and peoples concomitantly with the marginalisation of other areas excluded from privilege. It is this same argument that was used in dismantling the supposed privileges within the business sphere through a series of fiscal reforms which were in all respects punitive or meant to stifle their businesses.

The last aspect of the restructuring process was the creation of a new ethno-regional hegemonic alliance with the "Beti" at the dominant pole. In a series of reforms initially styled a *New Deal*, Biya regime reordered the hegemonic arrangement in favour of his own tribal base. As such, government, parliament, bureaucracy, the army, the police and the dominant sectors of the state were reordered to ensure a sweeping majority for the head of state's region which was progressively erected into a homogeneous tribal entity. It is a paradox therefore that in the name of redressing inequalities and privilege the regime created a new ethno-regional hegemony that was so sweeping that the process of associating other groups has been even less token or cosmetic than that of its predecessor[15]. This would make one believe that the critique of Ahidjo's regime and the idealisation of the intensions of the new Biya regime, presented in some cases as messianic, were rather just an alibi since the logic of the system was maintained and only gradually reconstituted to favour the new actors on the scene.

---

[15] A study such as the one undertaken by Ngayap (op. cit.) at the early period of Biya's regime is lacking but it would suffice to say that the hegemony exercised by the Beti is simply overwhelming in government (where they not only hold the strategic positions but also have a numerical majority), top governmental bureaucracy (where they exercise a near monopoly over administrative appointments) and the army and police (where they are the majority of commissioned officers as well as foot soldiers). In fact, this situation had become so evident by the late 1980s that the call for democratic reforms was also assimilated by other constituted ethno-regional blocks as a struggle against the Beti either in the direction of dismantling it or replacing it with another ethno-regional bock.

I have also shown elsewhere that the Sawa protests in the wake of local elections in 1996 led to an integration of the Sawa in the hegemonic alliance (Yenshu 2005, 2006). From a more formal standpoint the constitutional revision of 18 January 1996, which was the product of a debate that started with the clamour for democratic reforms, enshrined certain warped and clumsy clauses into the constitution in the name of addressing questions of ethnic imbalances within metropolitan areas. In fact the constitutional debate had taken place against the background of claims for the protection of minority rights both from constitutional/official linguistic minorities (the Anglophones) and peoples who had been relegated to the status of minorities by virtue of modernization/urbanization and the influx of non-natives within their once tribal homelands (the coastal region, Yaoundé) (Yenshu 1998, 2005, 2006; Menthong 1996; Tatah Mentan 1996) Although the constitutional claims of the Anglophones were more legitimate because based on a history of contracting between two territorial and demographic entities, the dominant voices in the constitution drafting process preferred to be rather responsive to the more localized minorities within the scope of an ideology of autochthony. As such, the preamble of the constitution proclaims that the state will protect minorities and the rights of autochthonous peoples, a clause which was used by some elites as they created a category known as "indigenous minorities" clearly in distinction to the Anglophone minority that had become a simple linguistic minority.

This ideology of autochthony became more explicit in clauses which were introduced as part of a decentralization reform. Art. 57(3) stipulates that the Regional Council is supposed to be headed by a personality of local origins ("*personnalité autochtone*") while the executive of the council has to reflect the sociological composition of the region. In fact, this clause had already been part of the laws regulating the conduct of local and parliamentary elections when they stipulated that candidates for elective positions within the list system had to reflect the sociological composition of the constituencies. What this meant was that representation did not reflect a viable political or developmental programme but was supposed to be a patchwork reflecting peopling rather than capacity to be responsive to social interests. What the clause on presidency of the regional councils did was to place *autochthony* as a principle above social interests. While such a principle did not pose problems in areas where population movements had not put local peoples into a marginal position, in the coastal areas and the capital this meant that non-natives were excluded permanently from such a position in favour of natives whatever the level of competence. This has also legitimized xenophobic attitudes from local elites who assimilate all forms of protest to the vandalism of non-natives bent on destroy the "beauty" of the metropolitan areas to which they are nothing but ungrateful guests. The constitutional revision of 1996 in this way went back on the gains of the national unity project which had been at the basis of both unplanned and planned displacement of peoples across the national territory and, in this way, legitimized the recourse to ethnic xenophobia in the popular imaginary. This so-called reform led to a confused situation in its early days as peoples who were products of migration and inter-community mixing for over fifty years were suddenly disenfranchised in their new "homes" despite the fact that they had been actively encouraged by the discourses of the national unity project of the Ahidjo days to be comfortable where they were[16]. Conversely, the national unity project itself came to be perceived by people in these regions as a ploy to marginalize them, this notwithstanding the fact that the processes that led to both dispossession and marginalisation were historically rooted (Yenshu 2005, 2006). The inscription in practice of the Sawa into the ethno-regional alliance arithmetic or formula operated according to this logic which only sought to reconstruct the corroding power base of the regime while cynically excluding others from participation (absence from government, disenfranchisement and xenophobia).

Universalist Imperatives vs. Particularistic Interests in State Formation

One can say that the various experiments have resulted in an extremely complex situation of ethnic uneasiness, restiveness, bitterness and low-intensity conflicts. Such an analysis is not to subscribe to the Hobbesian image of a war-of-each-against-all that one finds in Nyamnjoh's (1999) formula of "a country united by ethnic ambition". In order to understand the process of ethnicity and the role it plays in politics, it is important to understand the process through which it becomes a political construct, that is, a fact of politics. The error of most analysts is to assume that the present ethnic-political entities are either natural or the products of long-term

---

[16] In fact there were planned resettlement projects in sparsely populated areas with incentives as early as the third five year development plan (1971-76). Although some such projects were never a success they led to population movements to areas such as the Nkam division whose indigenes later subscribed to the xenophobic autochthony discourses and politics of the Sawa movement (Yenshu Vubo 1998).

historical processes that have almost become second nature. In this regard, one would need to make a conceptual distinction between the primordial historic community, invariably the product of the *longue durée*, which is at the basis of the ethnicity of the *ethnie*, and the *ethnie* as a political construct which generated the ethnicity of ethno-regionalism (Yenshu 2009). It is possible that certain historic communities take on themselves an ethno-political colour in the present context but history shows that where this takes place the two do not more coincide (Yenshu 2003). What I strive to show is that the present context of the ethno-regionalization of politics is the product of certain historical developments or processes generated by dominant groups (colonial authorities, holders of state power) but also appropriated by other actors (nascent political class in the decolonization process, local peoples in the post colonial phase, emerging bureaucratic elite in the postcolonial state). Hence the production and manipulation of an ethno-regional view of politics is as much the result of the creativity of dominant classes or groups as it is appropriated and becomes both part of the political imaginary of local peoples and the basis of practice as the norm. To illustrate this point I will refer the reader to the expectations of some Cameroonians during the second phase of the democratization process since the 1990s.

Failing to achieve a national base, the popular forces which had concentrated themselves in the south-western quadrant (Littoral, West, North West, South West) started arguing that since power had gone to the North and the South it was normal that the other peoples concede that power be transferred to the Grand West (itself a new construct). To the proponents of this option the ethno-regional artifice had become real and was the real driving force of politics within a newly constituted block had to be integrated. In this regard one can conclude that the idea of ethno-regional conception of power had achieved hegemony in the Gramscian sense only roughly four decades running from the late phase of colonialism into the three decades of independence even if only partially as this applied only to the actors on whom had been forced the logic of this system. Bourdieu explains this type of process by the fact that the state succeeds in inculcating certain categories of perception that it creates by a series of formal and informal mechanisms such that by a certain time what is perceived as real takes on an apparently natural character because the individual has been fashioned to perceive in that way (Bourdieu 1994: 107). That is not to say that this process goes without resistance: in fact, it is only achieved out of competition and struggles with competing hegemonic forces. One need not belabour the point about the artificiality of these blocks but rather trace their roots in the history of political practice - short as it may be. I have followed in this regard Bourdieu's model of the emergence of the state which aims at understanding the historical logic of the processes at the end of which a state takes a certain form because, as he argues, the processes inaugurate and establish certain social and mental structures adapted to them in a manner that some of the things acquire a natural character (Bourdieu 1994:105; 125-126). The development of the prevailing ethno-regional logic is a corollary of the development of a unique form of the state with specific practices that breed the malaise that can be observed.

The process through which ethno-regionalism developed was neither unidirectional nor in a void which could have made of it a smooth process. It was concomitant with other collective processes of an idealistic or utopian nature such as nationalism that was captured in the pan-Kamerun ideal. It was also parallel to the process of the universalistic creation of the state[17] through constitutionalism and legalism: federalism, administrative centralization, concentration of forms of capital in the state, organization of territorial space through the carving of administrative units, development of a bureaucracy etc. It was as well concomitant with the modernization of the state in all spheres (economy, culture, education, social structure etc). As such, the development of ethno-regionalism contradicted the utopian drive of radical nationalism as the former adopted the posture of the only alternative in a process where the latter was vilified. In the same way ethno-regionalism also thwarted and made a travesty of the enthusiasm of the UPC/Anglophone pan-Kamerun union movement as the ethno-regional drive entered into a contradictory clash with the universalistic posture of the new state. The same can be said of the process of modernization which became trapped in ethno-regional fetters. The resultant effect is a mix of contradictory processes that gives the appearance of a monstrous hybrid where utopian nationalism coexists with ethnic xenophobia, where the will to rational organization is undermined by a sectional competition in a perverted form of Norbert Elias calls the monopoly mechanism (Elias 1982) and where the drive to accumulate capital at this incipient stage as a means of laying the basis of a public space in the general interest is frustrated by the siphoning of collective capital to sectional interests. The process of creating a modern

---

[17] For a discussion of this phenomenon see chapter 4 ("Esprits d'Etat") of Bourdieu's *Raisons Pratiques*.

state in this case has become what Bruno Latour styles a characteristic modern process of the production of hybrids (Latour 1997: 68) without the accompanying process of the elimination of the hybrids that he observes in the West. The greatest distortion is the attempt to portray the struggle over power as the struggle between imaginary ethno-regional blocks. This distortion itself generates with it two forms of struggles. The first is the struggle within its own dynamic as it generates and sustains its own world (a struggle which we will call intra-systemic). This is the most rampant (civil wars, ethnic cleansing, ethnic competition over state resources) but also the most illusory and dangerous as history has shown. The second form is extra-systemic as the model is confronted by the pressures of the national and international environment that simply undermine the infrastructure and ideological base of ethno-regionalism.

Chapter Three

Language and the Linguistic Question in the Bicultural Project

If other social phenomena can easily fuse or dissolve into each other easily language is the one of the most impermeable, the most resilient to compromise and the most distinguishing feature of human communities in the tendency for human societies to acquire distinctive identities or adopt attitudes of particularism. It is therefore normal that language becomes a key factor in disputes in national communities where linguistic features are significant markers of difference. It is often said that old habits die hard. Language is the hardest to die evidently because it is the oldest form of human habits. The central question in our analysis here is: just how do human communities cope with language differences when in contact? More precisely, how has the Cameroon situation of two official languages of European extraction evolved in the midst of an extremely plural linguistic context of indigenous languages? What is going to follow is not a classical linguistic analysis myself not being a linguist by training. Neither am I attempting a complete sociolinguistic profile of language co-existence, my initiation into socio- or ethnolinguistics being rather summary. What I intend to do in this chapter is to propose, by way of conclusions from observations of a more general nature (macro-level), novel ways of understanding the language situation of Cameroon through the prism of its bicultural experience. In an analytical model which seeks to combine an understanding of the effects of policy with the logic of actors out of the confines of the state, I intend to demonstrate that the linguistic situation reflects the general context of patchwork or mix of hesitant policies and official manipulative practices, a bifurcated national existence and hybrids.

The Politics of Language: The Option and Experimentation with Bilingualism

The most evident official strategy that was adopted as a result of the union and which still lingers on is the option of bilingualism. It was – to use Ahidjo's words quoted above – adopted as a historical compromise to the imperative of "difference of language" (op. cit.) and was concomitant, at the beginning, with the imperative of the federation and the spirit of a "one – country – two - systems" policy. In operational terms, however, it functioned at federal level on the basis of either a crop of bilinguals who were trained specifically for the purpose or a corps of translators in a situation of near lack of linguistic intelligibility. At federated state levels the languages of the colonial extraction continued to operate in near isolation with virtually no communication with each other. What made matters more complicated was the rapid development of administrative structures (creation of bureaucracies and administrative units) operating in a near unilinear manner and the development of unilingual schools in each federated state. As such, the bilingual option came to imply functional elitist usage of two languages at the apex (central administration) and separate development of each language in its former colonial sphere. In that way, the problem of complicated language usage was a federal issue, that is, the problem of those who were in contact with the ensuing consequences in terms of managing the polity from the top. The eleven years of the federal experiment (peculiar in its centrist vision) saw a crystallisation of these trends which have persisted right into the fifth decade of the union.

The institution of the unitary state in 1972 did not put an end to this situation. Although it dissolved the plural form of the state (federalism), it left the plural mode of operation intact. Each territorial unit maintained its language of administration and its school system which produced and reproduced its future personnel by an expanded use of the language. The precipitated merger of the civil service, where state employees could work anywhere, meant that erstwhile monolinguals could work in areas where their language of initial training was never that of their new work places. This is true of English speaking peoples who were sent to the Francophone areas (especially Yaoundé) as of Francophones who had to move to the English-speaking side of the country. This also meant that the children of such persons had no option than to take up education in and they themselves worship in the languages of the churches in the new work places. This is precisely the dilemma born of the disorder in which the precipitated introduction of the so-called unitary state suddenly placed the average civil servant. So-called necessity of service thus led to some of the most brutish forms of linguistic confusion and symbolic violence ever orchestrated by a thoughtless socio-political transformation. Such confusion and symbolic violence often had as corollary animosity between linguistic communities when new comers with little or no competence in receiving language communities were virtually ridiculed or treated with scorn. The peculiar case of English-speaking Cameroonians is a case in point where the term "Anglo" was virtually synonymous with backwardness or awkwardness. The retort in the form of "frog" did not have the same import or effect as this was coming from a demographic minority.

This situation persisted right till the end of the Ahidjo era when opposition to such policies from an internal front in a context of the Cold War, which had contributed in a very significant way in streamlining political opinions world-wide, was simply impossible or at best lame. The disarticulating effect of this symbolic violence of a very particular sort was simply stultifying and spared none of the two communities in contact. Neither the original dreamers nor the new champions of the union project had anticipated or thought out ways of coping with the disastrous effect of this linguistic jumble. The French speaking community at different levels had to start coping with a language which they had not been used to or were never prepared to encounter. When it came to the English speaking officials and civil servants who had to move and work in Yaoundé it was a totally different issue. They had to cope with overbearing counterparts who were lost about what they considered a clumsy presence and the use of an alien language. The demographic equation simply played against them in an imbalance of forces as they were in the minority. To coax through a referendum that decreed equal citizenship and equality in language usage did not immediately translate into reality. The political obsession with outsmarting partners in negotiation had the rash consequences of generating processes of damaging psychological and social dimensions that have not been examined critically up till date.

Biya's regime took this situation as a given and has never thought of evaluating it in the manner of a politics of a *fait accompli* busy as it was with dismantling the patchwork of Ahidjo's political arithmetic. Besides occasional official directives on bilingualism (which are hardly enforced) and the operation of linguistic training centres whose prime role is to train monolingual civil servants and other interested persons in a second language (a strategy that is largely ineffective), the status quo ante of territorial confinement of official languages to their former colonial spheres and a tacit acceptance of bilingualism at apex level (in this case the level of central state institutions) has been allowed to operate albeit without a clear political stance. The declaration of attachment to the option of bilingualism by high ranking officials (President or Prime Minister) should be taken not as policy options per se but as the reproduction of discourses which have become part of habitual or normal administrative practice. To declare that the Cameroon government is attached to bilingualism without effective policies amounts to nothing else but political discourse except one were to consider the three dimensional option as a form of bilingualism. In practice this is unfortunately not the case.

La capitale du Cameroun, Yaoundé, est restée essentiellement française. Les Camerounais qui viennent des provinces anglaises pour y travailler ne peuvent s'y faire comprendre en anglais. Dans l'administration gouvernementale de Yaoundé, le français occupe une place prépondérante : les bilingues sont rares, même si le bilinguisme fait partie des critères d'embauche des fonctionnaires. Le bilinguisme institutionnel est plus visible sur les formulaires administratifs. Dans l'armée, seul le français est admis. Les anglophones et pidginophones doivent devenir bilingues. Dans l'administration régionale, l'anglais est utilisé couramment dans les provinces du Sud-Ouest et le Nord Ouest. Cependant, les fonctionnaires anglophones sont désavantagés s'ils ne connaissent pas le français parce qu'il leur sera impossible de poursuivre leur carrière après quelques années de service ; il en est de même pour les policiers. Les anglophones ne peuvent recourir à des services dans leur langue à l'échelle du pays, alors que les Francophones peuvent éventuellement le faire dans la partie anglophone...[18]

The Language of Administrative and Formal Economic Practices

In the ensuing confusion it is the language of daily administrative and formal economic practices that imposes itself. By this I mean not the symbolic system of language taken as a whole. I am referring more specifically to what the French will refer to as "langage" or the set of codes specific to a specific field as opposed to the total symbolic system of communication which is referred to as language. In this regard, we are referring here to the "langage administratif" or "langage des échanges économique formalisés". What will approximate the "langage" in English will be the notion of "register" but "registers" by being restricted to "vocabularies" exclude issues of usage. In this case, we are taking language use to stand for "langage" but in a more restricted sense.

---

[18] University of Laval http://www.tlfq.ulaval.ca/axl/afrique/cameroun.htm

The balance of forces in the administrative system of Cameroon imposes linguistic practices that are predominantly French. This imposition, which should not be confused with an official stance to which it is opposed or subverts, is the result of a generalized context of administrative practices in French or borrowed from the French. These practices which are replete in report writing, correspondences, terminologies, public speeches and verbal communication are a direct heritage of the French colonial situation and sustained through a heritage of administrators schooled principally in French either in France or in the so-called "grandes écoles" (clumsily translated into English as professional schools) with a predominantly French undertone. All levels of senior or intermediary administration are manned by such officials. Historically, the effect of this development was to institute French as the dominant language of administration. At the onset of the unitary state experience English-speaking Cameroons had to try to learn to communicate in French in a spirit of seeking to be administratively correct, however badly they did. Later on, they adopted exclusively French technical terminologies for which they gradually lost English equivalences. Finally, the practice of sending official correspondences to the English speaking provinces in French has only gone to compound the situation. The resultant effect is the modification of the language of administrators of English-speaking origins with the intrusion of French usages and terminologies. This goes far beyond to the community of businessmen whose language of transaction with governmental agencies (customs, taxation, contracts) has been completely modified with French terminologies and usages. The situation of the armed forces (army, police, gendarmerie, penitentiary) where the language of instruction, operation and command is exclusively French and where the assimilation of English speaking elements is at its most complete form constitutes the extreme forms of this process of linguistic intrusion (not to be confused with assimilation).

Despite the dominant position of English as a world language it has not had a corresponding pervasive effect. There are borrowings into French at official level but these are rare and translate more the effect of cosmopolitanism (with the cosmopolitans) than an imperative of circumstances as has been with the English-speaking administrative officials. Although it can be argued that the birth of a permanent translation culture and professionalism has at time facilitated communication, it has rather not been very helpful as some of the translations are just a travesty of meanings. The emergence of awareness to the use of English in the French-speaking community is late and timid but merits special attention when we will come to talk of the school.

The situation of the private sector is not different: given that the dominant class of businessmen is French-speaking and that the greater part of businesses are concentrated in the French speaking part of the country, the language of business at all levels is predominantly French. Businessmen who have chosen to restrict their business to the English speaking provinces (and they are comparatively fewer in number) operate in English. However, when they have to carry out transactions in the metropolises of the French speaking provinces (Douala, Yaoundé, Bafoussam) they have to resort to French. These remarks will also apply to all employees of companies that operate on either side of the linguistic divide.

Language in the Formal Learning Situation the School and Universities

The three dimensional perspective of the separate development of each language in its own ex-colonial sphere with a de facto bilingual centre has been replicated in the school system not without the habitual abandonment of idealistic projects. At the on-set when the effervescence of the union was still at its heat, an isolated experiment in bilingual education was undertaken in two grammar secondary schools set up in Buea and Yaoundé in the 1960s to recruit and train youngsters on an equal footing in English and French with foreign (French and Canadian) financial and technical assistance. This was apart from the unilingual educational systems that were already in operation either in the state grammar schools in the French speaking sphere (e.g. Lycée Leclerc, Lycée de Jeunes Filles) or the mission–run secondary schools. The near totality of primary schools (run by the federated states) continued to be monolingual throughout the federal experiment. In such, a situation the freshmen and undergraduates of the Federal University of Cameroon of the early 1960s were largely monolinguals. Palliative measures were thus taken to overcome the huddles by training each community of students in a second language, an experience that become a permanent feature of the University of Yaoundé till the 1980s.

Primary and Post-primary Schools

Although the experiment in bilingual education lasted till some time in the 1980s, it was isolated and never spread beyond the three schools. Its graduates were therefore a rare phenomenon whose experience the governments did not even follow-up. New state-sponsored schools were set up over the years along the lines of the monolingual education that had obtained from the beginning. As the schools multiplied and have become an essential aspect of each big village so has the parallel monolingual education become the practical reality despite the claims of bilingual education. New forms of bilingual schools have arisen which simply run parallel streams of either grammar or technical education for each linguistic community wherever the presence of persons of each community are substantial. Even the schools, which were instituted to operate on the basis of equal training in two languages, have resorted to this model. It has to be noted here that given the shallow depth training, learning in a second language, even when made obligatory, does not necessarily result in any competence in that second language.

University

The university situation presented the same fault lines and distortions that were observable at other levels. Firstly, by way of the sort of operational imperative that we observed with the public service and formal economic practices, the French language asserted and imposed itself (as it did in the intended elite schools) as the language of instruction. The reality of imbalance in teaching staff in favour of lecturers with training in French was the determining factor. It was the dominant language of teaching and learning in all departments, exception made of the English Modern Letters section and the Department of English Private Law which tended to operate like enclaves in a predominantly French speaking environment. Secondly students, who in the majority, had received their elementary and secondary education completely in only one language were expected to receive instruction in a completely new second language. This was true of youngsters of English-speaking extraction as of their French speaking counterparts but the brunt of the resulting symbolic violence and psychological repression was born by the former. The result was alienation for a vast majority of English-speaking youngsters who either sought for education elsewhere (when they could afford) or abandoned.

Education for English speaking youngsters in the University of Yaoundé then became either an up-hill task or a near impossibility. Statistics would show a concentration of the highest number of English speaking graduates in the "enclaves" (English Modern Letters, English Private Law) considerable numbers in Geography and History, staggering figures in the natural sciences (biology, physics-chemistry) and few cases in philosophy/sociology/psychology and the earth sciences. A similar situation obtained with the intended elites schools where the highest number of English speaking graduates have been restricted to the school (faculty) of medicine, the school of administration and magistracy (for obvious political reasons of balance), schools of agriculture and the higher teacher training college (Ecole Normale Supérieure) (for obvious operational reasons too). Cases of admission into the engineering schools (Polytechnique, Ecole de Travaux Publics) were rare for a long time although the situation has improved considerably. As such, vast areas of higher learning were shut off from ordinary English – speaking peoples from a technical point of view although in principle the doors of the university were open to everyone. In this regard, disciplines such as mathematics and computer science, public law, philosophy, German, Spanish, engineering and management tended to be considered as the preserve of the French- speaking community and no-go areas for Anglophone. In this way, one can comfortably conclude that there is a generational loss in the English speaking community with a mass of budding minds excluded from higher education by a brutish, thoughtless amalgamation. This does not exclude the fact that some English speaking students excelled and continued to become distinguished scholars, experts or administrators through the system[19]. All this occurred in spite of the presence of some of the best minds that have come from the English-speaking community and who have done an honour to Cameroon with their own achievements. The presence of the latter in key positions was instrumental in instilling certain positive traditions which have become a living legacy in the bicultural experiment. It is in this regard that one can mention the efforts of the pioneers and heirs of the project of the School of Health Sciences (now Faculty of Medicine and Biomedical Sciences) in moulding the institution

---

[19] I am a graduate of the University of Yaoundé system before the 1993 reform which saw the split of that university into six separate universities spread of the school.

into a neutral space of learning ready to benefit from the critical contributions of each academic tradition. Its history as well as that of its links shows that it has indiscriminately benefited from the groundwork of its founding fathers of both backgrounds (Monekoso, Eben Moussy, Anomah Ngu, Nguh Lifanji) which is a continuing legacy as well as the links it has continued to keep with Swiss, French, American and Belgian universities. It has accommodated its dons of both traditions without squabbles as it has accepted both the "aggrégation" and the English academic traditions.

Lastly, the situation in the then University of Yaoundé proper was totally different. The image one gathers is that of all attempts made to maintain the situation as long as the university lasted. There are no signs of alternative proposals anywhere as the lecturers who found themselves into teaching positions took the situation for granted. An attempt to restructure and remodel the degree programmes from a four-tier system to a three-tier system was abandoned in the manner of all harmonization projects. No sooner than later had the university started recruiting lecturers trained in the English traditions did there arise a quarrel over equivalences of certificates, a quarrel which seems not to have been laid to rest even with recent reforms[20]. The substance of the debate was that of understanding how university certificates obtained from a three-tier system could be equated with those from a four-tier system. Several solutions oscillated from political compromises, which lasted for a short while, through arbitrary equations to the moment when there is a tacit acceptance of a "one-state-two-systems approach": every certificate is valid on its own right. The paradox is that this anachronistic debate occurred till a moment when Cameroon was no more issuing four-tier degrees and when the Ministry of Higher Education is still carrying on exercises in equivalences for foreign degrees. The introduction of the BMD (Bachelors-Masters-Doctorate) system has put a temporal end to the debate but the shame is that it has come almost as a neo-colonial imperative when the reason is mimicry of the French in their integration into a pan-European initiative rather than a well-thought endogenous project in full awareness of the diversity of world systems. As a matter of fact it points only to the need to follow the European model while ignoring the demands of the American which still stands out as the most performing example. For now the BMD is still in its experimental stage and its results are yet to be felt.

---

[20] Paradoxically this quarrel was not reflected in the general civil service corps.

Award of scholarships to study in foreign universities with their differences in traditions between 1960 and the 1980s also went to crystallize these trends.

Post 1990 Developments and Impact on School/University System

The pro-democracy movement of the early 1990s had vibrant echoes in the lone University of Yaoundé when students took the lead in street marches to call for reforms. Within the university campus itself the protest movement found a solid expression in what its leaders called the Coordination of Students but which students popularly referred to as parliament (*parlement*). Teaching staff grouped under the National Trade Union of Higher Education Teachers (SYNES) also joined hands in requesting for reforms. Although extensive studies have been devoted to the study of this movement (Konings 2002, 1996, Konings and Nyamnjoh 2003), nothing seems to be devoted specifically to the issue of language instruction in the university but for open calls from dissident students of English expression for the setting up of a university of English expression. As a palliative to the pressure exerted by the protest movement, the government went ahead to create two more universities in 1992. This decree reverted to the logic of the one–state-two- systems approach by transforming the former Buea University Centre into a full-fledged university along English-speaking traditions (later on clumsily labelled "Anglo-Saxon") and the University Centre of Ngaoundere into a university along the French traditions. In February 1993 four more universities were created by transforming the university centres of Dschang and Douala into universities and splitting the University of Yaoundé into I and II. This brought the number of universities to six in the characteristic style of a tacit one-state-two-systems approach and a blurred, undefined middle course understood as an imperative of bilingualism.

As such, two universities ran along the lines of clear-cut monolingualism or bilingualism understood as the existence of two languages within the same territorial space (in exclusive but mutual co-existence) while four universities were declared to operate on the basis of the imperative of bilingualism. Not surprisingly, while the University of Buea (in the main) offered an opportunity to the English speaking monolinguals who now had an opportunity to escape the stultification, symbolic violence and alienation that largely characterized Yaoundé and Ngaoundere could operate a university without an ambiguous imperative of a second language (although the reality is different in the professional disciplines), the four other universities tended to replicate the former University of Yaoundé situation (de facto use of French as dominant language, confinement of use of English to Departments with relevance, low representation of English-speaking academic staff within the other departments). At global level, the functional imperative of French as the language of higher education administration has tended not to facilitate the situation but has rather contributed to subverting the gains of the 1993 higher education reforms and recent developments. Attempts to streamline academic practices within a harmonization scheme have met with little success and rather seem to undermine attempts by universities to chart fruitful autonomous paths. Even the qualifier of Anglo-Saxon used to refer to the University of Buea should be taken with caution because of the fact that it has its roots in the French usage of the word and would evidently have a different meaning in the American and British context. The University has tended to operate as an Anglo-American mix tapping from the American style in terms of structuring of syllabuses and teaching-evaluation practices (at least up to the modifications consequent on the introduction of the BMD) and the British system of administrative organization (highly influenced by practices in the other universities whose organization is inscribed within the overall administrative organization within the country). It is lacking to a great extent in terms of the autonomy that one would observe with universities in the English speaking world as there have been increasing attempts by the central authority to influence the structuring programmes in the name of harmonization and to dictate administrative practices as it is tied to the overall administrative system within the country.

The institution of experiments in monolingual university culture has its own benefits, namely giving the chance for a new experiment in how students can learn consistently in one language if adequately prepared in that language. This is a universal experience. Up till 1993, Cameroon was the only country in the world where a student could study in one language and suddenly be requested or compelled to study in another language for which he was not prepared to use. If the results of Buea and Ngaoundere are anything to go by they must be lauded. The desire to have university education in English at the University of Buea among French-speaking Cameroonians (a tenth of the regular applicants for some time) is eloquent proof of the benefits of a well-structured system. Conversely, quite a good number of English-speaking youngsters have succeeded to acquire certificates in the University of Ngaoundere. These remarks are besides the point of the relevance of monolingual education in a multilingual job market which we will examine later.

The trends of searching for functionally sound education at primary and secondary school levels in the language of the *other* linguistic community has become a fashionable trend (especially among the French-speaking elites) since the 1990s. Once characteristic almost exclusive of Anglophones, it is now very fashionable within a younger generation of Cameroonians. These trends which are proof of voluntary adaptations and cross-cultural mixing merit separate investigations of their own. For now, one can but point to their existence and the openings they provide. These are trends that are occurring outside official claims and slogans and operate according to the logic of non-state actors. Again the good example is not that of the politician and state officials but that of good-willed visionaries

Implications of the Developments on Education and Social Fabric: Imbalance and Imperial Feelings of Sufficiency

This distorted situation has not gone without its impact on education and social fabric. The first thing that comes to mind is the impact of the evolution of training patterns on the job market. On the whole this has been marked by strategies – however unconscious or unintended but real - of monopoly and effects of exclusion. As such, the bulk of competences trained within the country has followed the pattern of structuring and participation within the school systems as described above: sciences, technologies, management disciplines and certain key social sciences (philosophy, sociology, psychology) or certain modern languages (Spanish, German) have continued to be dominated or held in monopoly by French-speaking elite with the consequences of marginalisation and exclusion for English-speaking Cameroonians. This has implications in terms of access to the job market. Although it can be argued that this has been counterbalanced by privately sponsored education in the English speaking community, it has to be noted that this is essentially limited by financial means and further aggravated by the effect of exclusion by way of socio-economic background. The poor who cannot afford will not be in a place to gain access to positions where their counterparts of equal social standing in the other linguistic community would have. The resultant effect is a structural imbalance in the generation of technical competences such that the English-speaking community seems to be essentially backward with the implications that it has to be constantly assisted or dictated to in matters of expertise by a French-speaking elite not by virtue of competence but by the sheer argument of demography and the results of a skewed school situation.

The second implication (that is closely related to the first) is the loss in whole generations of talents at all levels especially higher education. The dissuading effect of education in a dominantly French speaking environment has had a heavy toll on English speaking Cameroonians for at least a generation. The few persons who succeeded are confined to disciplines that are practically peripheral. As such, on the average the average Anglophone who had a university education in Cameroon during the first three generations was sure to be a teacher, and thus confined to reproducing a class of teachers and the limited and limiting system of grammar education that obtained in the English speaking side of the country. This generational loss will take a very long time to fill and this can only be through very gigantic efforts that the current trends are only timidly addressing or redressing.

Thirdly, and closely related to the two preceding points, is the dwarfing of the English educational system for a long time at both primary and secondary school levels. This was primarily because of its inability to achieve continuity in a higher educational setting and which made the majority of its products to appear at best as good secondary-school leavers. The experience of the University of Buea with the acclaim that it has had in a relatively short time coupled with the flood in applications from school-leavers attests to this point. Even then, despite attempts to enlarge the scope of disciplines (e.g. managerial disciplines), it is still limited in terms of a broad-based university orientation. For now disciplines of some key social sciences (philosophy, psychology), modern and African languages, engineering, agriculture and until recently medicine are lacking. The explanation that is advanced in terms of lack of and a scarcity in competences (which still true holds for existing disciplines) can be partly explained by the pattern of training that the first generation of English-speaking Cameroonians had (as we have demonstrated above). Even the relatively considerable numbers of beneficiaries of government scholarships in the period 1960-1990 has not been able to ward off this dwarfed situation as many of the trainees on state scholarships did not turn to take jobs or were rebuffed on return. At the level of the secondary school the situation of a restricted grammar education until recently can be explained by a colonial heritage of missionary education which survived unaltered into the independent West Cameroon experience and has only been the subject of gradual changes of recent. Technical and commercial education was introduced officially principally during the on-set of the union and promoted by private business interests for close to three decades. Most of the private technical and commercial schools (e.g. Kamerun Technical College, City College of Commerce, Longla Commercial College, Providence Commercial College in Bamenda; City College of Commerce, Kumba; Vocational College of Science and Technology and Fess Technical College, Muyuka; Comprehensive High School, Limbe) and various institutes of secretaryship/stenography operated on programmes geared towards examinations set by academies in Britain (e.g. Royal Society of Arts, London Chamber of Commerce, Pitman Institute) and produced a crop of skilled workers in several fields. Progressively, either some of these schools have closed down for lack of relevance or have been caught in the fever of the fashion of grammar schools that was instituted by the two pioneer mission schools (Bali and Sasse Colleges). State sponsored technical education that set in after some time has evolved principally as an adjunct to technical education in the French-speaking section of the country with the setting up of the so-called technical colleges along the lines of the *collèges d'enseignement technique industriel et commercial (CETIC)* and *lycées techniques*. Reports are rife about the linguistic aberrations that result from teaching and examination practices in this context. Recent developments with the settings up of independent examination boards have been instrumental in improving this situation by expanding syllabuses and providing instruction or examinations in English. However, a lot more still needs to be done to go further into functional training especially in the technical disciplines.

With the French-speaking community, which is relatively shielded from the distortions of the system and which is the reference point rather than a victim, there appears to be a feeling of imperial sufficiency and lack of concern for development. It looks as if the language problem and that of the school system is not the concern of its elite. In one case, the willingness to accommodate English is only as a function of the state imperative to sanction bilingualism as an unshakable tenet of the polity. Bilingualism imposes itself in the schools because it is imposed by the state. On the other there are some elite whom are moving away from a system which has been unable to think and rethink itself. This explains why some French speaking parents are orientating their children towards the grammar school system of the English speaking part of the country. While the technical education system is productive in producing its crop of middle level technicians in a wide variety of trades, the broad nature of the programmes of the grammar school grouped into series seems to be largely a waste of students' time when there should have been specialisation early on at intermediate level (second cycle). Moreover, the institution of huddles at the intermediary level (the famous *probatoire* or eliminatory examination) has been the source of distress for many a French speaking Cameroonian.

This in-ward looking attitude in the French-speaking community is largely responsible for the situation in the university system that resulted in imbalances but also the inability for a whole generation of French-speaking Cameroonians to benefit from the association with an English culture. The development of cultures of cultural difference and indifference result from such an attitude. This does not imply that the structuring of teaching and learning has not had its own problems. At a time when Cameroon stands to gain from a bilingual situation it would be but myopic to continue to pride in an imperial posture. This imperial posturing by one community, on the one hand, and marginalization and exclusion of the other community on linguistic grounds, on the other, has had the unintended effect of bifurcating the academic community around an in-ward looking or cocooned cultural conflict over the intrinsic and extrinsic value of the educational sub-systems, which far from rapprochement, are overtly in competition. This relates to the modalities of teaching and learning as well as to the value of certificates. The latter is compounded by an official policy (largely misunderstood) of determining equivalences to or accrediting certificates obtained in universities outside the sphere of French culture. The bulk of persons affected by this situation are Anglophones. The resultant conflict is felt with resentment and anguish by all strata of the Anglophone intelligentsia and is translated in an ambivalent complex with both expressions of inferiority and claims of superiority. There is at the same time the claim of a better system and certificates which Francophones want to destroy or fail to acknowledge (superiority complex) and a ready willingness by same persons to implement directives by Francophone officials which undermine the very specificity of an English style (American or British) educational system of education and its certificates (inferiority complex). In this regard, the ambivalence translates itself in the same persons who are both critics and emulators of the same values. The same ambivalence translates itself in Anglophones who insist on giving English equivalences (this is outside the Ministry of Higher Education's office of equivalences) to degrees obtained in Yaoundé (rendered in French with some translation which does not matter to those bent on officious equivalences). Some Anglophone holders of these certificates who subscribe to this vision then have to go through a tortuous process of pursuing several years of repeated work so as to conform to this popular ideal such that an Anglophone who went through the then University of Yaoundé had to take, on the average, much more time than his Francophone counterpart or another person who followed a straight course in an English university. Some would spend fours years to have a "Doctorat de 3e cycle" and proceed to a Ph. D. to spend another four to six years (making ten years alone at doctoral level) at a time when their colleagues elsewhere would spend six years maximum to obtain a Ph. D. after a Master's degree. The best will even spend half of those years. The wise ones will take a Masters degree after the Maîtrise before going in for the Ph. D. All these gymnastics result from the reality of this asymmetrical situation of languages of instruction and educational systems resulting in domination, exclusion and reactions of ambivalence. These are partially issues of the past but they are important because they have impacted on whole generations of Cameroonians and are hard realities that must be faced. If an Anglophone student could sail through the University of Yaoundé conveniently at the first degree (and we have seen it was not), it was not the same for post graduate studies. Exceptions exist but life is not made of exceptions.

With the developments that usher both into novel forms of bilingual orientation for some (orientation of children into a second language to the received language) and the entrenchment of new official monolingual experiences for others, there is progress but progress in complexity. Just as there is a risk to produce monolinguals that may not be adapted to the multilingual situation, the new perfect bilinguals will be the hope for transforming Cameroon tomorrow. This points to new situations of inclusion and exclusion that are likely to develop. The imposition of bilingualism in public political discourses as an imperative for high state officials has no real effect as it is couched in its tokenism as political commitment does not often translate into practice even among policy makers and promoters.

Language in Popular Social Interactions and Informal Economic Exchange: Creative Multilingualisms

The *de facto* situation of obliged co-existence with speakers of two language received from separate colonial experiences has placed new types of exigencies on Cameroonians in their private encounters whether this is in the neighbourhoods, the markets, the extra-curricular situation (for the young), religious groups or entertainment (whether as producers or consumers). The situation of contact has become a complex and colourful one the more so with the presence of pidgin English and a multitude of indigenous languages numbering more than 250 languages. The general observation is that on the average, Cameroonians in the situation of contact of the two languages are multilinguals (speaking at least three languages) rather than simple bilinguals. In fact, each Cameroonian who has to come fact to face with another of another ethnic group will on the average use a native tongue and one language intelligible to more than two persons - not to talk of the misleading concept of lingua franca in this case. Lingua franca languages exist but they are regional: pidgin English in the south western quadrant (North West, South West, Littoral and West) to varying degrees and fulfudé to the North (Adamawa, North, Far North). Competence in the use of more than a combination of two languages will therefore be a function of literacy (closely linked to socio-economic status), exposure and the zone of contact. Literacy levels account for formalized forms of second language use (speech and writing) even in informal contexts while simple exposure accounts for the learning and use of pidgin English (or broken English) alongside broken French as a second language respectively. Both literacy and exposure account for different degrees of competence and use.

A geographical analysis of language contact and multiple language use would rather show a differential performance varying from very high to very low according to the degree of contact. The towns close to the linguistic divide are the most intense theatres of linguistic contact by virtue of population movements as a direct result of the migrations across the linguistic divide (depending on the degree of activities necessitating contact) and multilingualism in its most spontaneous (not to speak of natural) form. Douala (by far the most significant metropolitan centre), Bamenda, Bafoussam, Tiko, Buea, Limbe and all the important towns of the Mungo (Loum, Mbanga, Manjo, Nkongsamba, Penja, Melong) fall into this category (see map 1). In the situation, one does not only find multilinguals combining formal English and French with indigenous languages but novel sorts of bilinguals combining broken French and English, specific local forms of pidgin English and local languages. One should not forget that it is not only formal English that is in contact with formal French; pidgin and broken English are also in contact with various forms of informal spoken and broken French. The situation of Yaoundé is specific because of its imperative as capital that hosts workers of the two linguistic communities as well as migrant workers. Its level of multilingualism will therefore follow the same pattern as the geographical zones of intense contact.

The situation becomes more monolingual (actually bilingual when one adds the local languages) in one of the received languages as one moves away from these zones of concentration. The phenomenon of strict monolingualism in either pidgin English or French in the urban areas needs to be investigated but it is a reality. Reinforced with monolingual training in the formal school situation this becomes a serious handicap in a multilingual situation. In quantitative terms therefore a considerable of proportion of people are multilingual in a variety of combinations but a lot more are likely to be strict monolingual in the use of a received language restricting them to imperfect bilinguals in the use of their native tongues and a receive language. For an effective language policy there is a need to carry out a linguistic survey in this direction.

A linguistic mix (créolités to borrow from Amselle) has arisen from the creative intercultural borrowings that the situation of contact has imposed. Research points to the persistence of such trends as embodied in codes that have been styled *camfranglais* or *francanglais* (as the case may be) although they are minimal and restricted to certain forms of colloquial speech among the youth.

Figure 1: Diagrams showing overlapping of Educated English (EdE) and pidgin English (PE)[21]

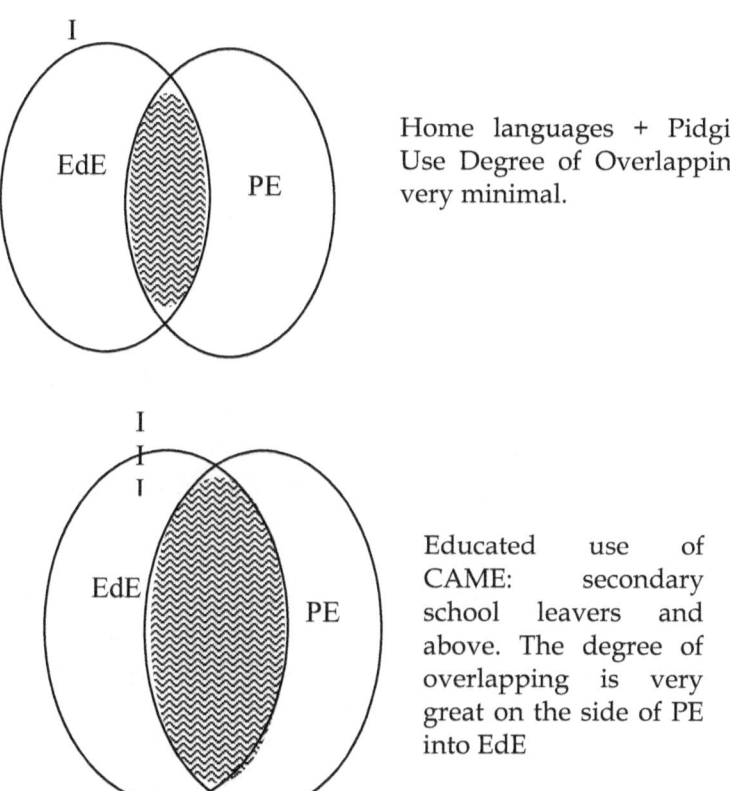

Home languages + Pidgin Use Degree of Overlapping very minimal.

Educated use of CAME: secondary school leavers and above. The degree of overlapping is very great on the side of PE into EdE

---

[21] These diagrams are verbatim copies of diagrams made by Mbassi-Manga (1976).

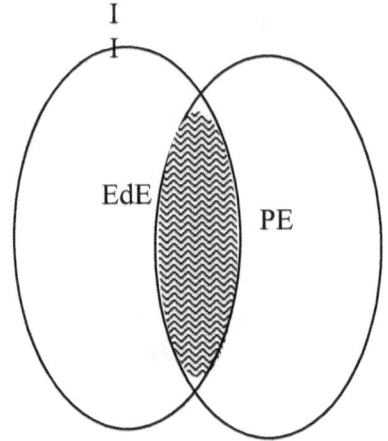

Cameroonians having attended only primary schools. The degree of overlapping is fairly significant.

Conclusions

Three situations have generated three trends which largely determine the conclusions one can draw. Firstly, the official linguistic position is that of declared bilingualism but the context of official administrative practices, characterized by a history of one-sided integration of personnel of English-speaking origin into French inspired traditions and linguistic practices, makes for the domination of French as the language of administration and the pervasion of certain usages ("langage") derived from French to the extent that current English terminologies in Cameroon are but transliterations (in opposition to proper translations).[22] The assertion and imposition of French has not been total or complete as it is limited by the imperative of bilingualism, which, even token, puts a check to the complete hegemony of the French language. A second scenario consists of the operation of parallel systems of monolingual primary and secondary education (which account for the reproduction of parallel monolingualism and the assertion/institution of parallel monolingual university education (amidst a continuing assertion of French as dominant university language and the persistence of French-inspired practices as the model). This second scenario in the school system is also characterized by substantial and significant cases of parents orientating their children into a second language education (i.e. second language to a

---

[22] The case of Cameroon is not unique but can be observed in situations where certain language forms occupy a dominant situation vis-à-vis others.

formalized home language). It has to be noted that official attempts to experiment effective bilingual education failed and were abandoned. The official attitude currently is to simply teach a second language alongside the first in all schools. The third scenario is a cosmopolitan situation which cultivates various forms of teaming multilingualism but which is limited geographically to the contiguous territories across the linguistic divide and the national capital, the contacts characterized by intense cross-boarder population movements. This situation is contrasted with a situation of generalized indifference to the presence of the other received language as one moves away from these zones.

Confluence of ethno-linguistic reality, transethnicity and linguistic cultural contact in modern context of Cameroon

Situation 1: Cosmopolitan areas of Yaoundé and Douala

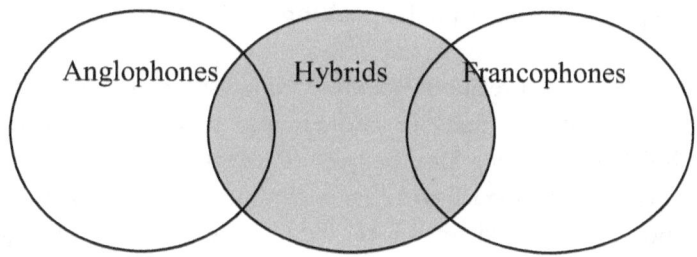

Hybrids at the centre

The grand linguistic divide between English speaking and French speaking communities is overarching in relations. Some local peoples live in near total isolation with little or no contacts with others although there is also a core centre with intense contacts. The core centre is where one would find most hybrids. This is the situation of Yaoundé and Douala.

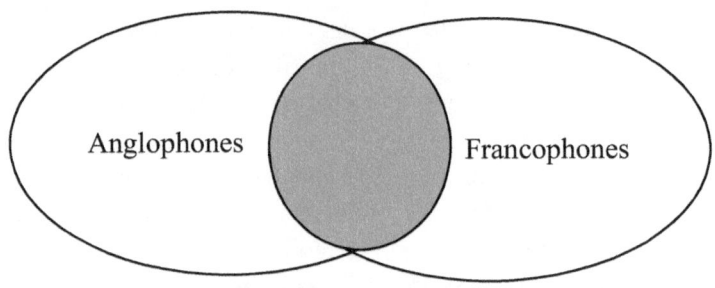

Hybrids at the centre

The grand linguistic divide between English speaking and French speaking communities is overarching in relations. Some local peoples live in near total isolation with little or no contacts with others although there is also a core centre with intense contacts. The core centre is where one would find most hybrids. This is the situation of Yaoundé and Douala.

Situation 2: Hybrids at the borderline areas between predominantly English speaking and French speaking territories.

New intercultural relations across the linguistic divide lead to new forms of creative adaptation that are grafted unto preexisting intersections and trans-ethnicities involving local peoples. There is extreme cultural *metissage* or mixing. The monolingualism / monoculturalism of colonial origins is superimposed or grafted unto local cultures in new creative ways. Foreign languages influence local cultures while local cultures conversely impact on received languages and cultures (situation 3 below and map).

Situation 3: Foreign culture meets local cultures which are intersecting.

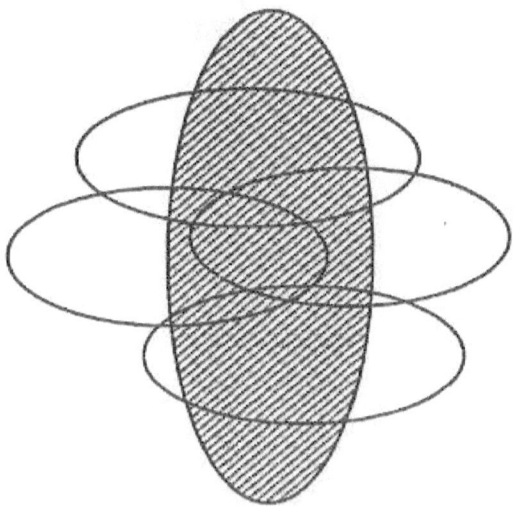

The overall image projected by this situation is one of a plural linguistic and cultural order characterized by the emergence of autonomous subsystems evolving in relative insulation/isolation from each other. In terms of official policy, there appears to be an impasse except for the occasional sloganeering around the commitment to bilingualism which has become a ritual part of official discourses. The latter, in effect, appears in reality more as a minimalist approach left to the actors to accomplish depending on the eventual usefulness of a second language to the person involved. One can also conclude that from the degree of success so far the task of building a bilingual country is just simply enormous and that the attitudes of policy makers is a cowardly resignation and refusal to face the reality which has just simply become increasingly complicated. There is therefore a need to realistically redefine the contours of a new linguistic policy that will solve both the puzzle of the bilingual situation in clear-cut terms and the complications arising from the development of nearly half a century of coexistence. In such a situation, one would have to face the issues of whether bilingualism is necessary for everybody, whether or not to redefine bilingualism (may be as one-country two languages in different spheres) and where to put indigenous languages and *lingua franca* (which pose specific problems of their own). At a time when current trends move towards countries opening up to the learning of second languages (as is the case of Nigeria and Madagascar) and which would have put Cameroon in a leadership position due to its bilingual situation, it is actually a pity that leaders have opted for a politics of retreat into linguistic cocoons.

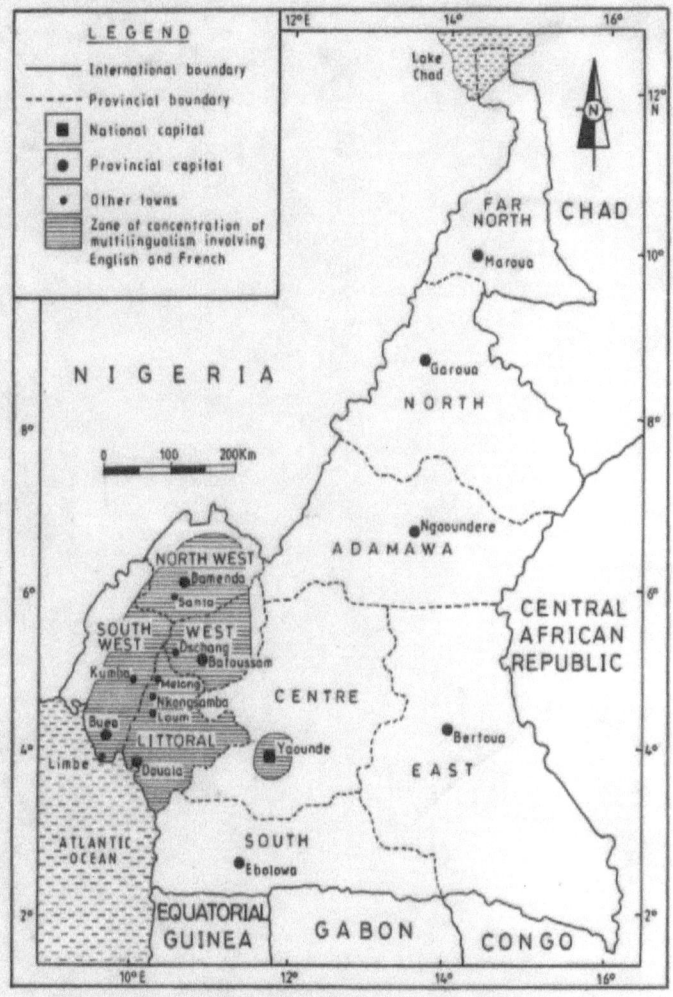

Fig. 2: Map of Cameroon showing zone of concentration of intense linguistic plurality and contact.

Chapter Four

Between Assimilation and Roll Back In Harmonisation Projects

One of the contentious issues which have bedevilled Cameroon since the onset of the union experience is the question of harmonization of certain core areas of public life, which by dint of their differentiating nature, tended to necessitate or place an imperative on consensual mergers. The prime concern here is with some of those areas where harmonization was either overtly or covertly attempted or implemented, and the fate of the harmonization projects. These core domains are the administration, the armed forces (army, policy, gendarmerie, penitentiary), the legal system and education. The argument is that, while harmonization in the army has been total (by absorption) and dominantly in favour of French in administration (but for certain token concessions), harmonization attempts in the legal system and education have been rather characterized by hesitant steps and roll-back. The hypothesis we are advancing is that while all areas are sensitive, the harmonization of the armed forces administration/culture and the civilian administration was achieved in the same manner as the forced political order in the context of asymmetrical negotiations and inconclusive arrangements as a way of forestalling separatist strategies. The failure to achieve same in education and the legal system is due to resistances borne of entrenched habits instilled by the federal experience. These explanations are evidently opposed to the essentialist explanations which pit a so-called Anglo-Saxon culture against a Gallic culture with which it is said to be in compatible (Nkwi 2004; Awasom 2004). Given that the cultures are essentially European with a core of underlying values derived from a common heritage (deriving from Greek antiquity, Roman/Latin Legislation, Renaissance, Enlightenment, political and cultural revolutions from 16th to 20th century), it would be largely erroneous to pit them in an essentialist frame of absolute incompatibility. This is proof of a cocooned frame of thinking that confuses one's immediate world with the whole world. It is not simply ethnocentrism or even sociocentrism but a misplaced frame of both. For one thing it would be wrong to judge the relation between French and English civilizations from the narrow frame of the Cameroonian situation.

What we hope to achieve here is to describe how these processes became possible and the reasons for the outcomes.

The Armed Forces

As with all the other sectors of public life administration and armed forces followed different paths or patterns during the federal interlude. The federated state of East Cameroon inherited the structure of the French colonial administration and its army, police and gendarmerie, and continued to build on them especially in the context of the conflict with UPC forces which had resorted to arms principally in Bassa and Bamileke country. It had also received extensive French assistance (as the independent French-speaking Republic of Cameroon) to build up its armed forces which was one geared principally towards repression in a context of conflict with an internal insurrection. This was backed by several accords of "Cooperation and Mutual Assistance" between the newly independent country and the ex-colonial power (in reality legal instruments crafted to counter the UPC uprising through French backed military force). The result was the build up of a ferocious mixture of an army with an essentially internal mission of pacification, that is the repression of insurrection of an armed sort, an essentially anti-people police with a mission of stifling liberties and surveillance of dissent (secret police) in the name of a "Raison d'Etat" (state logic) and a paramilitary force (gendarmerie) whose place in the hierarchy of armed forces is not clear except that of covering of rural areas (hide outs for the insurgents) through surveillance of communication routes, identification of persons in transit and investigation of criminal cases[23]. The emergence of this situation and its stabilization in the federal interlude accounts for the development of a tradition of repression which has survived beyond that period into the contemporary history of Cameroon and which merits its own separate investigation. Suffice it to mention the practice of arbitrary arrest without warrant, collective searches and street arrests without warrant (the infamous "callé callé"), the blatant use of public torture on suspects, the use of naked force against protesters, the omnipresent and pervading presence of a secret police (SEDOC, CENER etc) and its special detention centres (BMM) with a dreaded capital in Yaoundé, the tracking down and detention

---

[23] Note has to be taken of the fact that the gendarmerie was itself born in France itself during the period of the Vendée insurrection during the French Revolution.

(accompanied by and dehumanized treatment) or forcing into exile of political opponents and dissenters and periodic raids into suspected areas of rebellion.

This did not go without its own impact on judicial procedures. The state and its agents were force of law or the law itself. It was no more incumbent on the state and its agents (the complainant) to prove an accusation before the law but the accused were bound to prove their innocence. The logic was that a powerful state could not be brought to prove what it was saying. At the same time that this enhanced the powers of the investigating officers (gendarmerie, police), it reduced the powers of the judiciary as an arm of government which could not in all independence arbitrate. It is therefore at this time that the imbalance in arms of the state (in favour of the executive) – the judiciary was just an authority and not power while the legislative was transformed into a mirror image of the dominant figure whose members it hand picked (Yenshu 2006:169) - can be traced and not to an essentially Gallican nature of institutions derived from the French Cameroons as some researchers have asserted without very convincing proof (Awasom 2004). The repressive apparatus of the state thus became a powerful tool in fashioning an overbearing central structure dominated by an executive devoted to the person of the President. The absence of a structure of armed forces representative of a federal level implied that the armed forces derived from the newly independent Republic of Cameroon were transposed to the federal and national level.

In the federated state of West Cameroon, the situation was totally different. Having received no formal structure or repressive state apparatus from the British, the short period of internal government (1954-1961) being rather marked by continuous dependence on Nigeria in the main, the new federated state of Cameroon had to set up its police and an associated paramilitary force (mobile wing), evidently to the limits of acceptability within the union. The impression is that of at token force which did not achieve full expression (it was concentrated in a few of the urban centres then) by the time the union was dismantled through the manipulation that ushered in the unitary state. Some unrecorded sources point to the threat of the paramilitary force as a reason for the character of harmonization process. That is unlikely for two reasons. The first and obvious is that the structure of this police force was still rudimentary and could not pose a real threat of armed resistance. Rumours of importation of arms with a view to resisting an impending unitary state have also been circulated but even secret service documents seem to be mute on this. This needs to be investigated. The second reason which is obvious too is that a unitary state could not go without a unified and single armed force structure. This was an imperative that is incumbent on every state. The question is just how this was done.

The process of harmonization after 1972 was characterized by an integration of the skeletal police force of the federated state of West Cameroon into the police force in East Cameron (equally taken to represent the federal police) and the progressive recruitment of Anglophone into the army and gendarmerie through the appointment of some of its key officials to the General Delegation for the Police in Yaoundé and the absorption of its elements into the regular structure and corps of the police force. As for the army and its paramilitary wing (gendarmerie), in a spirit of nationalization of the army, it proceeded to recruit Anglophone massively as it integrated the staff who had served either as commissioned or non-commissioned officers in the colonial army when Southern Cameroon was administered with Nigeria. The absorption and recruitment of English speaking soldiers, police men and gendarmes into a monolingual armed forces structures along the line of French tradition and evolving in peculiar historical circumstances made for the imposition of the latter's language and practices (both formal and informal). The language of command and the practices have survived as inherited from this period as have reforms that are restricted to this logic.

The territorial organization of these forces (army legion or command units, gendarmerie legions and brigades, police delegations and districts) has made for the deployment of this monolingual structure throughout the territory not without its own peculiar consequences. While the *modus operandi* of the armed forces has been evidently French in the French-speaking provinces (even for Anglophone officers), the situation in the Anglophone provinces is peculiar. While one would encounter monolingual Francophones who only work in French (and would argue that Cameroon is bilingual), the imperative imposes bilingualism for persons whose first received language is French. Such bilingualism would evidently contrast with bilingualism in two received language in formal situations (administrative usage, correspondences) and bilingualism in French and the lingua franca, Pidgin English, in informal situations where monolingualism in one received language is the rule. A clear example is that of the traffic police or gendarmes who fruitlessly try to impose French only to resort to using Pidgin English as a working tool.

The Administration

At the administrative level, during the federal experiment the two federated states ran two administrative systems, the one being a direct continuation of the French colonial structure with its *régions, départements, districts* (number) and *cantons* while the other sustained the partition of its territory along the same lines as the reorganization exercise of the late 1940s which had broken up the former Southern Cameroons into divisions (six in number) (see Yenshu Vubo 2006).. The two federated states all had state-level governmental structures (with legislative, judiciary arm and executive arms) with some token autonomy in some spheres although they were financially dependent on the central level for survival (Chem-Langhee op. cit.: 21 -22). In all this gave the impression that this was a good model to continue. Presumed guarantees – in what we termed above asymmetrical negotiation and inconclusive arrangement – were to the chief architect of this system, President Ahidjo but a temporal measure in the road to a unitary state (Chem-Langhee ibid: 21). Scholars of a psychologistic school advance a blame theory which attributes the dismantling of this administrative structure on the malfunctioning of the federated state of West Cameroon and the political wranglings of its politicians (Ngoh 1999; Ngoh et al. 2004). This is to be oblivious of the political developments that led to this process. There was largely a consensus across the whole spectrum of West Cameroon politicians (although for entirely different and opposed reasons): politicians in government who wanted to consolidate positions played to Ahidjo's intentions of abrogating the federal experiment while those excluded acquiesced to the same plan as a way of escaping the system of competitive politics which had succeeded in West Cameroon by rendering them irrelevant (see Mbile 2000). A cardinal reason that is often advanced is the role that the imbalance in wages played in mobilizing the civil servants to the very idea of a common civil service. It has been reported amply that the civil servants of the West Cameroon state were eager to be on the same salary scale as counterparts in East Cameroon whose salaries at the same level as those of federal civil servants. This is the crucial factor that warded off possible resistance to the integration-by-absorption scheme. Moreover, moving over to the capital, also federal capital and capital of the former ex – French-speaking Republic of Cameroon, would carry with it opportunities for enhanced administrative and political positions. As with the army, the coincidence of federal administrative services and style of functioning with the administration of East Cameroon ushered in a situation where movement towards national level also meant integrating into a that type of administration with its practices.

From the angle of administrative organisation, an early strategy of reordering within the perspective of homogenising (that would usher in the unintended effect of ethno-regionalisation) was to reorder the new Cameroon along what was known as regions (precursors of the current provinces). Its function instituted and equated the West Cameroon state with one of the six regions of the federation and thus gave the latter an ambiguous status as both a state and a region with conflicting powers to two sets of officials (regional federal inspectors of regions appointed from the centre and elected officials at the federated state level). It is at this stage that one has to situate the process of un-negotiated harmonization by administrative dictate (i.e. decrees) and not later on. In this regard the administrative downsizing of the federated state of West Cameroon was a process of strategically structuring units of similar demography weight to contain them in a scheme that would splinter the south into considerably small units and leave a gigantic North which would not be challenged by any unified south within the politics of northern domination to which Ahidjo was committed following in the footsteps of the colonial administration.

This dichotomy was also accompanied in practice by a disconnection of the two regions as there were no attempts to create regular means of communication between the two segments of the country. In the partitioning of administrative units that accompanied the unitary state, the logic of ethnic exclusion played a dominant role. It has to be noted that the zoning into provinces institutionalized the regional model that had undercut or had been overlapping with the federal structure. The politics of regional ordering was consciously meant to create regional consciousness of an ethnic type both from within an internal and external perspective. Inhabitants of a province would thus see themselves as specific and see others as specific to their own provinces. It is my opinion that that this largely accounts for the development of the perception of Anglophones by Francophones as an ethno-regional grouping that can be equated with other ethno-regional groupings and not as a constitutionally distinct category.

The subsequent institution of provinces in 1975 only went to confirm this logic when seven provinces were created with five in the Francophone area corresponding roughly to the five regions of 1962 and two deriving from a partition of West Cameroon along the lines of the British partition of

Southern Cameroons into a Bamenda Province and a Cameroon Provinces in 1949 (see above). From a macro-sociological perspective, both the process of the referendum and its ensuing decrees had achieved a process of administrative harmonization from a spatial level as each administrative unit was equal to the other in statutory terms although in real terms imbalances continued to subsist. Further divisions into smaller units - although carrying different nomenclatures - were practically ordered from the centre according to the uniform principles of a top-down automatic administrative streamlining. Even the reordering in size of some of these units in the Biya regime has not altered the logic while the training of personnel in schools situated at central level with uniform principles has only helped to solidify this situation. The institution of administrative services at the level of the new administrative units has been an important corollary of this harmonisation by decree and administrative dictate.

In the partitioning of administrative units that accompanied the unitary state, the logic of ethnic exclusion played a dominant role. It has to be noted that the zoning into provinces institutionalised the regional model that had undercut or had been overlapping with the federal structure. In all, the partitioning was hegemonic and meant to ensure allegiance to the regime. The division of Anglophone Cameroon into two provinces corresponded to the Bamenda vs. Cameroons Provinces division of the late 1940s, this division being largely meant to forestall the Anglophone acting as a single block in the direction of secession in the same way as Biafra had done in Nigeria although the Northern Fulbe jealously clung to the myth of their unity. Many facts point to a sustained policy of disarticulation which favoured elites as against regional development and general welfare. Firstly there was a devaluation of the capital of the former federated state to that of a provincial capital accompanied by the development of rival centres (Bamenda, Kumba) and exclusion of areas that had voted against the unification option (Wum, Nkambe, Mamfe). Secondly, there was an intensification of the divide born of the KNDP government's balance sheet of exclusionary politics. For example, former KNDP elements continued to monopolize key positions attributed to Anglophones in the ethno-regional arrangement.

The provisional West Cameroon representatives in the Federal Government, the Federal National Assembly and the Diplomatic Service were all from the KNDP. In West Cameroon, the members of the West Cameroon Government and all top-level administrative appointments were held by KNDP members but for the short-lived coalition of A. N. Jua (Ngoh 2011: 92).

Thirdly, the Anglophone region was disconnected by a sheer neglect of intra-regional communication networks (Mamfe-Kumba; Bamenda–Mamfe) as the new administrative units (provinces) were connected more to the new provinces in the French sphere (Littoral, West Provinces), a fact which has continued to be the source of deep suspicion from autonomists who consider this an attempt to simply merge English speaking into the Francophone provinces.[24] In fact, the idea of integration has always been interpreted to mean annexation (Ngoh ibid.: 75).

The so-called policy of regional equilibrium in administration and development was often a smokescreen behind the political arithmetic of trade-offs in a situation of imbalance. In practice one could notice that the persistence of the nationalist critique as well as a growing discontent expressed in a governance-centred critique resulted in a dichotomy between pro-regime and anti-regime elites within the same region this corroding the mirage of claimed regional unity and representation. Secondly, there was a division between regions tagged as pro-regime and others tagged anti-regime, a fact which destroyed the myth of regional balance based on artificially designated regions. For example, when certain logics of affirmative action favoured the Anglophone and Northerners as lagging behind in modern schooling or the Bamileke in a trade-off to exclude them from politics, this only resulted in discontent in areas where alleged favours were not accorded. According to Biyiti Bi Essam (op. cit.: 87), this meant slowing down those regions considered to be advanced and pushing ahead others considered backward. What went in the name of balance, whether administrative or developmental, was symbolic or token. There was a general appearance of all regions participating in government but this was in fact an arrangement where a few hand picked politicians stood for regions. Intra-regional conflicts between elites competing for power or intra-regional hegemonies are glaring contradictions within the scheme.

---

[24] This is bolstered by the fact that certain services (the central bank's regional offices, headquarters of military command region) meant for the North West or South West Provinces are situated in the Francophone provinces.

The Justice System in Cameroon: A Mix of Structures

The justice system presents an image of a mix of harmonisation of structures, a stalled process of harmonisation at the level of practices and procedures leading to a de facto *one-country-two-systems* approach and a situation of outright monopolies (by Francophones) within certain legal professions (notaries, bailiffs). Although the harmonisation process has been rather half-hearted, protracted and marked by forward-backward movements, it has yielded some significant advances either by the administrative imposition for the most part or by consensus in very limited instances.

By 1964, two Federal Law Reform Commissions had been created to draw up a Penal Code, a Criminal Procedure Code and several other Codes. Its only achievement was the 1967 Penal Code which remains the only reasonably successful legislation that reflects the country's dual legal culture, although it was substantially based on the French Penal Code. Based on the unitary Constitution of 1972, Ordinance no.72/4 of August 26, 1972, which has since been amended several times, created a civilian- style unitary system of Courts to replace the different court structures that had operated in the two states (Fombad 2007).

Structural harmonization is characterized by the following:

- A uniform structure of the magistracy along the lines of a single streamlined administrative structure. This is based on a single magistracy trained in the same school, the Ecole nationale d'Administration et de Magistrature, and which, on graduation is integrated into the same structure. It is also governed by a uniform system of promotions and rewards. There is also a single corps of registrars with the same structural characteristics. According to Fombad (ibid).

The courts within the country operate within a unified but decentralized court structure at the summit of which is a single Supreme Court for the whole country that operates more like the French *Cour de Cassation* rather than an English Court of Appeal. The highest court within each of the provinces is the Appeal Court.

This centralization is concomitant with the process of administrative and political centralization in the unitary state instituted in 1992.

- There is also a single bar unified under one canopy, the Cameroon Bar Association (Barreau du Cameroon) with a democratic structure that makes for the possibility for each member to be eligible to any elective position irrespective of linguistic origins. (Trace History).

- There is a single structure of investigation and law enforcement officers (state counsels/procurators, police, gendarmerie, penitentiary) with uniform principles and practices (applications and abuses) all over the national territory, a fact which gives a distinctive imprint to the justice system.

- All legislation has been codified either into laws, decrees and ordinances that are applicable to all Cameroonians although there are still references to "received law". Feh (2009) reports references to "Enactments by the English Colonial Legislative Authority" and "The statutes of general application in force in England as of January 1, 1900" as characteristics of the English received Law in Cameroon as opposed to "Enactments by the French Colonial Legislative Authority" applicable in Francophone Cameroon. The very idea of reception of laws is the source of legal confusion. The legal system (as the educational system) has refused to autonomously think itself as an instrument of independence. It either stagnates paralysed by its cultural warfare between Anglophones and Francophones or only reacts in relation to international fashions. There has thus arisen an uncoordinated mixture of codified laws in the main (as in civil law) and bifurcated practices (civil procedure vs. Common Law). As such, the claim to difference (case law or civil law) is in the process of adjudication than in the substance itself. Case law itself is rather limited in its application as in references to precedence to proceedings in Anglophone Cameroon. Fombad (op.cit.) has argued that:

> The English legal system on which the law applied in the Anglophone provinces is based treats judicial precedent differently from the way the French civil law on which the law applied in the Francophone provinces is based. The English law doctrine of binding precedent or *stare decisis* under which judicial precedent is a major source of law was received in the Anglophone provinces as part of the general reception of English law. Its actual operation to render judicial precedent an effective source of Cameroonian law is however subject to the complexities of the judicial organization of the courts in the country.

For the two Anglophone provinces, the doctrine of binding precedent operates in the sense that the precedents laid down within each province constitute binding authority within that province. However, judicial precedent as a binding source of law in the English provinces plays but a rather limited role because of the "provincialized" system. Although appeals may be taken from the Court of Appeal to the Supreme Court, these are not usually handled as appeals in the strict sense of the word and the decisions taken by the Supreme Court are at best only of persuasive authority. To this extent, whilst judicial precedents remain important source of law in the Anglophone provinces, because of the way the courts are structured and actually operate, it may not be as significant as it should have been.

The concept of heritage is also challengeable on several grounds. Besides being a crippling idea, it reflects a sort of "self-colonization" that refuses to free its adherents. In reality, it is not a reproduction of a received culture[25] as it is presented in official parlance but proof of the leadership's inability to rethink a system that is adapted to local reality as well as a reflection of the tendency to "invent traditions" (cf. Hobsbawm and Rangers 1992) of difference as the only political solution to the difficulties posed by the union. In sum, there has been a general tendency not to engage in a critical collective examination of the state as a way of providing it with a rational, legitimate and autonomous basis. By referring in this regard to the heritage of colonialism as the sole basis for founding its plural composition (bilingualism, bi-jural system, biculturalism), the successive regimes miss the chance of creating a genuinely independent and unique state by transferring the cultural base to an externality.

- Lastly, there is a uniform procedure for initiating and enacting laws.

Divergences are observable at the level of procedure and practices that have continued to reflect a colonial heritage. Although lawyers are free to practice anywhere in the country, the magistrates are practically always assigned to practice in the area of their competence in a received language and, by extension, received procedures. As such, although one would find Anglophone lawyers in Douala and Yaoundé (although the reverse in not

---

[25] It is doubtful that the Laws that are presented as received were applicable to locals during the colonial era given that there were clear distinctions (with legal implications) in colonial territories between citizens of the colonizing powers and subjects (natives in the English sphere, "indigenes" in the French) as has been explained extensively by Mamdani (1996). As such, the native or customary courts were reserved for locals while the modern ones heard cases relating to citizens. There are doubts as to whether this is what is meant by colonial heritage. It is rather a shameless transposition of that never held sway during the colonial regime.

true of Francophones in Anglophone Cameroon), the magistrates in these towns are mostly French-speaking. All magistrates are trained in the same school but practice in different systems: a common law tradition (based on case law) in the English-speaking provinces and a civil law procedure of French inspiration in the French speaking province. (Investigate what happens with English speaking lawyers in Yaoundé and Douala). These divergences are the result of bi-jural practices.

Legal practice has also been largely affected the history of decolonization and independence. In the context of transfer of power at independence characterised by armed resistance from the UPC and accompanied by repression, summary executions and a dominant executive justice became a top-down affair where notions of fair judgment were largely absent. Repressive laws too restrictive of individual liberties were passed at this moment, the powers of the executive enlarged at the expense of the judiciary which has been dwarfed since then and exorbitant powers granted to law enforcement and investigating officers (police, gendarmerie, customs officers, prison guards).This will explain the meddling of the Executive in matters of adjudication and the administration of justice (the judiciary is run in this regard by a ministerial department and the chief executive also chair of the supreme council of the magistracy) as well as the characteristic arbitrariness of the police, paramilitary officers and the army in matters of investigation and law enforcement. It is also true that these trends are a prolongation of the brutality of French colonial brutality in the post-World War II phase of colonialism and in reaction to calls for independence (Benot op. cit.). This was the paradox of the "modernized" (Benot ibid.: 53) or "enlightened" (van Nieuwenhuizje 1983: 30) colonialism. It was in this light that postcolonial governments inherited the colonial habit of magistrates acting more like police officers.

> A la vérité, le corps judiciaire aux colonies en 1947 (et dans certains cas en 1950) est fort différent de celui de la métropole. /In all honesty, the judiciary in the colonies in 1947 (and to some extent in 1950) is different from that in the metropolis (Benot op. cit. : 122)
>
> Les mœurs de la magistrature coloniale sont décidément plus proches de la police que de la justice/The ways of colonial magistracy were closer to those of the police than those of the justice department (ibid. : 149)

In the absence of a corps of properly trained magistrates the colonial practice of creating magistrates out of court registrars and civil servants (ibid: 123) became the rule in the early days of independence. It is in this way, that the repressive attitudes of late colonialism were transferred and assimilated by the new elites in an uncritical manner in the name of heritage.

Monopolies can be found in some professions that are not well-developed or absent from the English speaking provinces such as the sheriff-bailiffs and notaries. The former was for a long time monopolized by French speaking Cameroonians to the extent that the first set of professionals to practice in English-speaking Cameroon were French-speaking and monopolized extensive jurisdiction way beyond legal stipulations. This has resulted in a situation where this profession has resulted into an excusive club dominated in the main by French-speaking Cameroonians even when some Anglophones gain access into the professions. The profession of notary, on its part, has been the exclusive club of the Francophones. The underdevelopment of these professions in English-speaking Cameroon can be explained by their history in French speaking Cameroon and the strategies of monopoly but also by the habit of English speaking lawyers combining the seemingly diverse functions of advocates, solicitors, notaries and sheriff-bailiffs. In the absence of a legal framework which gives room for such practices, the open ground has been filled and is monopolized by Francophones.

The general observation that one gathers is that of a mix of practices that combine uniform practices, bi-jural procedures and practices and monopolies of key sectors all these controlled by a diversity of institutions: several ministries (justice, police, gendarmerie), Supreme Court and President (as Supreme Magistrate and President of the Magistracy Council)[1]. The situation becomes more complicated with the alignment of Cameroon to uniform Acts that are applicable to principally French speaking countries (CIMA code, OHADA). Barrister Akere Muna has argued that:

> In as much as one may claim that a ratified treaty takes precedence over internal laws and the constitution, one cannot reasonably require the courts and jurisdictions to apply laws in a language that one does not understand. The translations of the Uniform Acts are literary and less

---

[1] One needs to investigate whether the idea of placing the President at the head of this institution is not part of the devaluation process consequent on the crafting of institutions to the advantage of the executive arm.

adequate. They do not translate known legal notions of the Common Law system and allow most common Law judges and Legal Practitioners to apply this new law by a sheer approximation. In case where there is simply no equivalent, courts in the Common Law jurisdiction have continued to apply pre-OHADA laws which have been abrogated (Muna 2004: 10).

It is in this regard that Tumnde is of the opinion that in the process of adhering international treaties of this type "the bi-jural nature of the country ought to be preserved and promoted. Any meaningful reform should take into consideration Cameroon's national peculiarities".

At best, the situation which prevails in Cameroon is a plural legal order which is characterized by a largely uniform structure and content of law and enforcement, differences in adjudication processes (procedures) and a *de facto* situation of monopolies in certain legal professions. Feh (op. cit.) feels, on his part, that:

> Today, modern Cameroon municipal law is a hybrid, indeed a modified version of the received laws, peculiarly adapted to its Cameroon environment. Moreover, it is, also a novel blend of local and imported laws and international treaties, harmonized and integrated together. In other words, we are witnessing the emergence of a new species of Common plus Civil Law, a specifically Cameroonian Common/Civil law defined, fortified and elaborated by local legislation and decisions of Cameroonian courts.

There are evident problems in such a situation. For instance, the dominant role of certain investigating officers especially in matters concerning the state (public order, political dissent known at some time as subversion, crime) undermined a procedure that was based on presumption of innocence applicable (the "accusatory" dimension cf. Feh op. cit.) in the English-speaking provinces before the harmonisation of the Criminal Procedure Code. Cases of suspects transferred from one jurisdiction to another by order of procurators in order to favour particular types of procedures in judgment are proof of this trend. The Uniform Acts with an international dimension also poses problems of procedure in English speaking courts: are local courts to be left out in adjudication on matters deriving from their jurisdiction? How did monopolies evolve and how are these monopolies to be disentangled? What is the fate of mono-cultural legal procedures existing side-by-side in a parallel manner in a single national territory? These are matters that need detailed investigation and concrete realistic solutions.

Primary and Secondary Education: Continuous Asymmetry in Understanding and the Reproduction of Difference and Identity

Reproduction and Expansion of Colonial Culture

Forty years of colonial rule in during the League of Nations and later United Nations mandate in Cameroon witnessed two different styles of attitudes towards education. As we mentioned above in relation to manpower development, the French had embarked on its own form of training its colonial subjects. In consonance with practices in other colonies, there was a commitment of training an *évolué* class of a subaltern corps of indigenous civil servants (the famous "commis") who were to occupy a middle position between the colonial administration proper and the natives (indigènes) in a tradition that has been misconstrued as a general policy of assimilation. This thus dictated the type of public schools that were to be set up and the nature of the curriculum to be taught in these public schools. A number of public schools at both elementary and post-primary (secondary school and teacher-training college) level were set up as early as the 1930s. The Christian missions also ran their own schools whose syllabuses in secular training were subject to vetting from the colonial authorities. It is from this structure that the class of elites who led the independence movement was drawn (either in its radical or compromise form). Brilliant students on graduation either from the secondary school (whichever section) could also gain quick access to French scholarships to study in French university institutions or specialized schools. As such, the school system was fashioned closely to the system of Indirect Rule or what Amselle calls indirect administration (i.e. associating indigenes in the management of colonial affairs) which consisted of consciously creating an *évolué* class (see Azeyeh 1998). This created its own peculiar situation of ambivalence as the first persons to challenge colonial rule (and in the most radical manner) came from this class as was also the case of faithful servants of the colonial administration (the famous *"interlocuteurs valables"*). By the 1940s there was already a teaming class of *évolué* concentrated around the coastal peoples in particular (Austen and Derrick 1999; Derrick 1989) and generally in the south of the country, a situation that was to generate regional differentials in school attendance figures and literacy levels in the new French speaking Republic of Cameroon (see Tables 1 & 2 below). This detail will help us to understand the internal structural problems of the emerging French-speaking component of a union that started as a federation.

Education in Southern Cameroons was limited to public and mission primary schools and two secondary schools run by the Christian missions (Presbyterian Basel Mission, Roman Catholic Mission)[26]. The content of this education was not evidently meant – from the colonial point of view – for even a subaltern position within a colonial administration. At best from an official policy level it looked like a segregationist system for a few natives who would serve (if they were ever associated) at the very lowest rungs of colonial administration since the indirect rule formula in the administration was left to the few officials from Eastern Nigeria (Ibo or Efik/Calabar). The only openings for teacher training or post-secondary education were in Eastern Nigeria (Yaba College of Technology, Hope Waddell, etc). Even then, the Christian missions produced their first graduates only in the mid-forties and had not produced any significant mass of enlightened natives by independence. One only has to observe the calibre of politicians to understand the school situation. It has to be noted that the content of teaching (manuals, text books) and style reflected a dependency on the Nigerian colonial situation. It does not come out clearly anywhere that the internal government did very much to reverse the situation or improve on it.

---

[26] For detailed analysis of the colonial situation see also Courade and Courade (1977).

Table 1. Enrolment in Primary and Secondary Schools in French Administered Cameroons

Year	Number of Schools		Enrolment	
	Primary	Secondary	Primary	Secondary
1947	137	3	18600	704
1951	203	3	28594	908
1956	583	5	79363	1479
1961	977	20	151635	4742

Source: Tchombe (2001)

Table 2: Enrolment in Primary and Secondary Schools in British administered Southern Cameroons

Year	Number of Schools		Enrolment	
	Primary	Secondary	Primary	Secondary
1947	229	1	25000	130
1951	266	2	28960	322
1956	385	3	46754	468
1961	449	6	86257	903

Source: Tchombe (2001)

The option of Southern Cameroons to join the independent Republic of Cameroon came as a brutal intervention in these two processes that were on independent/divergent paths and whose new managers were least prepared to handle. The speed of events and imperatives of political expediency did not also facilitate issues as the political agenda gained both precedence and primacy. The easy solution and the most obvious was to follow the lines traced by the federal model that had been adopted in broad outline but which operated only as a skeleton subverted by a drive towards centralization. Elementary as the development of the educational systems were – despite evident disproportions in quantitative terms – the architect of the new state opted to perpetuate the school system as initiated by the colonial powers (cf. Courade and Courade op. cit.). That is the substance of the option for a parallel structure, for it is at this is time that many more public schools were created along the system of colonial French education as the first public secondary schools and many more public primary schools were opened and multiplied along the lines of a general education that reflected the model of the mission-run schools in the English speaking section of the country. The experiment in bilingual education was very limited as we have indicated earlier. As early attempts at harmonization were stalled by misunderstandings and misgivings each sphere continued to replicate its colonial model in the name of identity and difference. In the federated state of West Cameroon, primary and secondary schools continued to use text books not only produced in Nigeria but ones that reflected the content of Nigerian realities for disciplines with a social content (English language and literature, Geography , Arithmetic and Mathematics) right till the late 1970s. The rest of the books were either produced in Nigeria, Britain or former British colonies (East Africa, Ghana, Sierra Leone). Although the Southern Cameroons had detached itself from Nigeria, it was paradoxically tied to this ex-British colony culturally through an educational system whose content was produced by Nigerians in the main for Nigerians with Nigerian realities. The replication of the missionary model - prompted initially by the need to train clerks – was equally copied and expanded to the detriment of a more balanced educational system in terms of streams (witness the marginalized sector of technical, commercial and vocational education). The major crisis that the development of this system has posed is not the threat of assimilation by Francophone elite whose system of education itself is in crisis and of which they are aware (witness the number of children the very wealthy Francophones or those in top positions orientate into English education). It is the internal logic itself whose daunting interrogation is: education for what? On its own it is too general and meant only for the brightest who can go farthest. Drop-outs are unable to pursue occupations and fruitful careers and are often forced to take on paths that this education did not predestine them for. Such a system needs a cure but it cannot have this cure alone because the job market is a single market.

In an attempt to balance its own internal regional disparities the French speaking side totally forgot to critically examine the heritage it was sanctioning and expanding by making it available to areas to which it had not reached in the colonial period in the name of regional balance that had become a pillar of the regime politics[27]. The structure of the primary and secondary school systems has remained the same despite its failure to deliver the goods. Although content (in terms of the *imaginaire* of the social disciplines) has changed considerably, the logic of operation seems to be out of tune with modern pedagogic trends and the realities of Cameroon[28]. The drop out rates are abnormally high in the secondary schools while the maintenance of intermediary structures (such as the *Probatoire*) is simple pushing parents and the youngsters alike to search for refuge in alternative sources of education considered viable or a safety valve: enrolment in English speaking schools (which has even become an aristocratic or bourgeois option), recourse to schools in Nigeria or enrolment for the *Probatoire* examination in Tchad or the Central African Republic. These indicators, some of which have become an eyesore to Cameroonians (witness the *probatoire* crisis or scandal of the 1990s), point to a crisis of the system.

The daunting question is: why has harmonization failed? The question would look surprising to Anglophones who have put up an attitude of resistance to what appears to be Francophone attempts at assimilation. The logical follow up to this attitude is not to be surprised at even the possibility of harmonization. If it ever happens, Cameroon will not be the officially multicultural country with a harmonized system of education: Switzerland, Canada and Belgium are glaring examples. The point is that the issue of harmonization has often been wrongly put, namely in the frame of a cultural conflict or competition of systems. This can be attributed to be entrenched habits of the parallel experiences that are becoming normal and the political experiences of forced political order that has only engendered bitterness. There is thus total lack of communication between the successive managers of the two systems to the extent that the only way out is to sanction the two stream system as a political given (see law No. 98/004 of 14 April 1998 to lay down guidelines for Education in Cameroon). Political expediency may dictate such options but training is not only a political issue (the production and reproduction of citizens), it is also an economic issue. Just how training is adapted to markets is as important as respecting the identity of citizens. Harmonisation issues, moreover, are issues of planning and planning needs expertise. In Cameroon, expertise was lacking at the beginning; at present the

---

[27] Very often the balancing was to the advantage of the North, President Ahidjo's region of origin (see Biyiti Bi Essam 1984).
[28] On the language component of curriculum see Fandio (2003).

expertise is too politically motivated to undertake the reform movement that can usher in a unified and balanced educational system.

In examining the linguistic question and the question of the human equation of employment, I have amply dealt with the imbalance in the structures of the former University of Yaoundé and how this was alienating for the general student population but very deeply alienating specifically for Anglophones. The decentralisation of the University of Yaoundé had no sooner ushered in the *de facto* plural order of separate parallel educational systems alongside an implied but blurred bilingual universities operating all on the Yaoundé model than did the temptation of harmonization set in[29]. It is not clear what the objectives to be achieved were: standardization of content or alignment of form? Neither of the two has been achieved because, although programmes were approved after the grand seminar of 2000 to the effect, each university continued to run its own programmes (different in content), structure (modular vs. course credit system) and administrative set up. The University of Buea, which gave the Anglophone intellectual elite the possibility (or Bourdieu's fields of the possible – *"espaces des possibles"*) to prove its own worth in an alternative system to what obtained prior to 1993, has been successful in initiating and keeping standards of academic performance and management to sufficiently good levels that it has been openly praised by all and attracts students from all over the country. As mentioned above, its scope still reflects the former orientation of the Anglophone community largely marginalized from some key disciplines in the humanities, social sciences and technology. For now, it still looks largely as a University of Arts and Science. The Yaoundé model (functional in some of the universities) with its tendency towards symbolic violence (intellectual brutalisation through an exclusionary examination system) and exclusion (not only on the linguistic minority) excels as a system of system maintenance where performances have been traditionally low, drop out rates high and teaching lax. The pedagogic objective of the teachers in some cases seems to be an attempt rather to exclude and assert the knowing position of the lecturers that must be maintained than an enhancement of the knowing capacity of learners. The diversity of the programmes is one of the very strong points of this system as is its tuning to practical and employment needs. In this respect, it is much in tune with many a modern educational

---

[29] University reforms are the subject of a separate study (Yenshu Vubo forthcoming).

system. Its greatest flaw is mystification and its tendency to the formation of social classes/differences.

The overall picture is a situation where the shock of contact by way of consensual desire to disagree on model of education has led to an easy but dysfunctional option. None of the systems is functioning optimally but none of the principal actors seems to agree on this. The collapse of the public school system for one is a glaring reality (statistics of GCE, Baccalaureat, University, FSLC/CEPE which does not even have certificates). This reality compounds the confusion that the refuge in private schools (even for the same managers of the public system) does not solve. In short, the attitude is one of irresponsibility where the public schools are left to deteriorate to irretrievable levels. Policy seems to be elusive as attested by flowery policy statements and objectives while evaluation sidesteps the realities of the market for which students are trained.

There is a clear recession of English as an official language despite declared bilingualism accompanied by a progressive corruption of the English language at popular level under the presence of French through intrusions and faulty translations. This is the result of official usages that are dominantly in French. The presence of Pidgin English is also blamed but this is a false debate. Difficulties in learning English are also the result of the so-called English-subsystem of education. The curriculum has no central supervisory body as teaching and learning is left in the hands of different actors: state-run schools, Christian missions and individuals ("lay private"). Each sorts of develops its teaching scheme with supervision from state official but a central curriculum level does not exist. This explains why the public schools where official programmes are supposed to be taught and follow up ensured are in clear decline. There is also a concomitant resort by parents to private schools because of their excellence. The paradox is that even state officials across the linguistic divide are attracted by such a sector which is both restrictive (by dint of its prohibitive costs) and elitist (producing elites and open to the elites). In such a context, the standards are maintained outside the official framework which is abandoned to itself. Language is at the centre of this bifurcation within a sub-system left in the hands of the English-speaking elite. The way public schools function also makes for much of ineffective teaching and learning: there is an urban bias amongst teachers working in the state institutions. Even then, laxity and poor remuneration are contributing factors. It has been observed that some of the teachers also effectively teach in the private schools where they are even more dedicated than in the institutions to which they are posted.

The puzzle that has to be solved is just how a plural educational system can train for a single job market. This refers to the question of the content of training and its relation to the job market. To reduce it to that of identity is to confuse life issues to identity issues. What is needed in the educational system is the acquisition and enrichment of mental aptitudes irrespective of linguistic barriers. When the French-speaking parent opts to orientate a child into the English stream the competence the child gets enriches the child but does not change the identity of the child in ethnic or geo-linguistic terms. What I am implying here is that the issue of reforming an educational system cannot be reduced to that of reproducing an identity and the solution of an identity crisis. In fact, the two issues can be isolated and treated separately each in its own right. In this regard, the same content of education can be taught to the same persons within the same frame but in different languages since the basic difference is linguistic. Most academic disciplines (Science, the Arts, engineering, medicine) have the same content and can be taught with the *same weighting in the same country*. In order for there to be equity one should not have the same graduates at any level with different orientations because this makes for imbalances in open markets. Furthermore, it can be advanced that the state could make available (either by provisioning or by giving incentives to other stakeholders) on an equal basis, as diverse a gamut of training fields as possible to all citizens who wish to pursue any system in his/her language of competence. The argument of cost can be advanced (as it was to dismantle the very experience of a political federation) but this is a vital field within which to invest and invest properly. The concentration of training in one language or within the geographical sphere of one language breeds with it the dysfunctions currently at work. A reasonable approach may be to implement such proportionately.

For this to be possible, the elite (intellectuals, state officials, politicians) have to operate an intellectual adjustment that breaks with the inward-looking frame of thinking that is bred and fed by the conflicts and misunderstandings between French speaking and English speaking elite. The effect of the inward-looking perspective (Bourdieu's *"effet d'enfermement"*), characteristic of the debate on education can only lead to myopia and a skewed reading of what, otherwise, are even global trends. For instance, many Anglophones have read the recent developments in Europe towards a Bachelor–Masters-Doctorate (BMD or LMD in French) as a triumph of an

"Anglo-Saxon" system without placing it in the context of the unification of the European social and economic systems of which the development is but a corollary. The analogy is that if France, alongside with other countries, is aligning itself to adopt a three-tier system, then French-speaking Cameroonians are wrong in imposing an anachronistic French-inspired system. That is missing the point in the internal logic of phasing out intermediary degrees (undergraduate and post-graduate diplomas in all systems). Again the French speaking elite has borrowed, under the imperative of belonging to the CEMAC zone as well as the CAMES and in a style characteristic of constant adjustment to changes in the ex-colonial metropolis (even when these changes imply France's other international engagements and do not involve the former colonies directly[30]), the discussion of the BMD as an imperative and it has become habitual discourse. It is often forgotten that, under the exigencies of the bicultural experience Cameroon was even a precursor by instituting a three-tier system (a *Licence* or Bachelor's degree, a Master's degree and a Doctorate). Although in principle this system functioned for some years (Master's and some Ph.D. degrees were actually awarded), it was scrapped and the elite relapsed into an anachronistic cultural war (value of systems, worth of degrees, equivalences, etc). In this period of relapse and confusion, it was the ordinary Cameroonian student who was the loser. Neither misplaced triumphalism nor a mimetic attitude born of the inward looking attitude will be a way forward. On the contrary, it is the source of stagnation and regression. There is a need to transcend this self-confinement within a narrow conceptual frame as a way forward.

In the process there will be a need to dissociate, both in practical and in theoretical terms, the cultural concerns (here education) and the political, even if temporarily. This will be important in understanding the importance of the cultural sphere to economic concerns of production (labour market, human capital building in management, entrepreneurship, consumption habits) as vital individual and collective (communities, state) issues. It need not be emphasized here that for now the cultural concern has been confined to the identity or political dimensions of citizenship. The livelihood issues only emerge in a peripheral manner although the latter are essentially what breeds discontent: the inability to procure jobs within the polity are a result

---

[30] Witness the worries over the institution of the European monetary union for which France was a key advocate and stakeholder and the alignment of the CFA automatically to the *Euro* as France became part of the union.

of lack of opportunities but are more the result of the inadequacy of systems of education that have not transcended the logic of self-reproduction geared largely towards the satisfaction of a quarrel over identities. The rising army of youth without a future made up of successful graduates of all levels as well as drop outs from the system (Jua 2003: 15) is symptomatic of the situation and is more explosive than any secessionist bid. The regular youngster ready to engage in any violent street protest (whether they are concerned or not) as a way of venting discontent or the readiness to expatriate to any country (I mean any!) is more the result of malaise related to employment and livelihood than anything else. When once the cultural question of reforming and adapting educational systems to common economic concern has been settled then there can be a return to the question of identity which will but be partially resolved.

Lastly, stakeholders in the educational system (managers of the educational system, policy makers, teachers, parents, opinion leaders) have to bear in mind that current trends are in the competitiveness of nations in which the ability of the educational system to usher in a viable productive tissue plays a central role. It is not the competition in the intrinsic values of the system per se because each system strives to produce the best of itself. Contrary to the narrow vision that is being promoted by some of the most successful English-speaking intellectuals which presents the world situation in essentially binary terms (English vs. French), there is actually a wide gamut of educational systems each arguing the validity of its internal logic. The logics of convergence that one finds today is not just a dictate of the lure of a brilliant Anglo-American model (which has its own internal divergences too), it is principally the result of the dictates of the market, principally convergence to face the exigencies of highly competitive production and market system. In some respects, the attachment to certain academic traditions and resistance to global streamlining is even not just a matter of academic nationalism; it is as a result of the fact that a system has proved its worth in a global competitive market. However, progress within a system is only thanks to its own internal critique and reforms that either derive from this critique or are a function of selective borrowing towards enrichment. It is not the competitiveness of factions of a nation that are likely to bring viability to its educational system. As we have seen, the absence of consensus only leads to easy solutions with no progress in view. It is therefore incumbent for Cameroonians to embark on a sustained critique of its system(s) of education, engage in discussions which imply a conscious stabilization of content (by consensus on syllabi) and structure (consensus on single system of weighting and duration of training). The substantial differences world then be only on language of training. In the process planners will have to learn from other successful systems around the globe.

Chapter Five

Towards An Anthropology of Conviviality and a Politics of Possibilities

The peculiar situation of Cameroon and its development necessitate an anthropology of conviviality within its polity. This anthropology will be comprehensive as it implies an analysis of all social dimensions of the polity (politics, economy, social relations, culture, language) that shape conviviality. The principal question is: how does the ordinary citizen live this situation of plural linguistic order (imposed, contrived or generated), politics between forced order and relations of domination/marginalisation, forced harmonized practices and roll-back in certain cultural fields? The ordinary citizen is not an exclusive category; he/she is the person in a situation which implies the contact between two citizens as ordinary agents outside official situations. In this case, a state official who has to buy from a local market is confronted with the local linguistic situation which imposes certain demands on him/her pitting his/her competence in the language in use with that of the trader. As such, an official becomes an ordinary citizen, despite the imposing dimension of his/her personality just in the same way as a farmer who is buying from the same market. I am not concerned here with the vertical dimension proper which would evidently be important in such ordinary interactions. I am more concerned with the horizontal dimensions of contact resulting from contact across peoples although in such an analysis the vertical dimensions will evidently come into play as issues of inequality are involved. In a way, the two are often combined into couples of horizontal-vertical differences where horizontal differences are structured vertically. In other words what originally is symmetrical in statutorily equal terms or stands in a face to-face relationship soon becomes symmetrically opposed in unequal terms. It is therefore important to identify these levels of unequal symmetry in the analysis.

Models of Conviviality

Before proceeding, it will be instructive to reflect on models of intercultural and inter-community contact. I refer to the two concepts of inter-cultural and inter-community contact because very often they are dissociated and culture treated as if it was existing on its own. That is the essence of a reified model of culture that treats it as if it existed outside the society or community of people with whom it is identified. This model should be understood as one which will function either in forced, consensual or involuntary/accidental situations. Forced situations are those of conquest (colonial or otherwise) or hegemonic drives by one part of the community on another or other. Consensual situation range from the agreement of a group to merge with others (integration) or the agreement of a variety of communities to live within the same political space subject to the same order (federation, confederations).

Involuntary or accidental situations are the result of pure contingency bringing peoples of different origins within the same vast territorial space in a contiguous manner. These different situations are characterized by different forms of convivial or relations. Forced situations are characterized by pure imposition and inequality in social relations. The harmony of situations of forced order is only achieved through brutal subjection by the dominant group and the imposition of rule and culture (even if that culture is only a poor variant of the dominant culture). Historically, this is the case of colonisations and nation-building projects in some European states that result in what I have termed elsewhere a model of cultural superimposition/replacement model (Yenshu Vubo 2006:216), the source of various forms resistance and hybrids at the level of lived experiences.

Consensual situations deriving from voluntary agreement to merge with others may lead to loss in identity especially if the in-coming communities were small enough to be absorbed into the dominant cultures. Some incoming communities may continue to express specific traits of their original cultures alongside adherence to the dominant cultures. This is observed in the incipient stages of the formation of heterogeneous ethnic communities or in communities of immigrants in the modern nation-states that operate an open-door policy to immigration. The latter is true of Hispanics and people of Italian origin in the USA as well as the Arab communities in France. At some point, the crisis of this bicultural (not to be confused with double allegiance) attachment becomes a critical issue in national life to the extent that it has to become official when it is recognised as official policy (as is the case with multicultural states). Other consensual contexts involving communities of people with substantially large populations but territorially situated within the same national space has resulted in a multicultural arrangement through political contracting. This is the case of the federal and confederate arrangements of Switzerland, Belgium and Canada which I have termed a contract model.

Contingency situations, which can be observed with the formation of ethnic peoples or modern nation states, have fluctuated between three poles: harmony, collaboration, cooperation; conflict, confrontation, animosity; accommodation. Harmony/collaboration/cooperation finds its expression philosophies of peace, expressions of good neighbourliness and fraternity, trans-ethnic and trans-cultural arrangements, bonding, treaties, pacts, ententes, internationalisms at both primordial and planetary levels, cosmopolitanism and forms of symmetry. Conflict, confrontation and animosity are characterized by philosophies of belligerence (witness its modern forms in the definition of others as Evil Empires or Axes of Evil[31]), expression and even exacerbation of difference, bickering over resources and positioning, confrontation, animosity and forms of symmetry or dissymmetry. Accommodation is a middle point between the two others and points to strategies of adjustment than to golden compromises. It is expressed in ambivalent situations of cooperation and competition, conflict and tolerance, enmity and fraternity.

All these situations are not neat distinctions in history; neither has any one set of societies exhibited only one of such characteristics at any times. Long periods of war, tensions and conflict may be followed by other periods of accommodation or prolonged periods of harmony. There may also be a mix where several forms of inter-communal relations co-exist even with apparently contradictory ones. For example, there may be conflict at global level but at substratum level there are forms of harmonious dealings such as "cross border" marriages, trade relations, friendship bonds, participation in trans-cultural forms of life (association life, the imaginary) etc. The globalising of society as one which discrete segments (e. g. Anglophone and Francophone) could be involved globally in a total conflict all the time with each other is often belied by these undercurrents of conviviality. In situations characterized by stalemates there may be no "official" relations between communities but at the same time peoples are committed to a conception of peace or equilibrium they may not want to overturn. In the case of modern nation-states these mixes become the more complex as they touch on both

---

[31] Witness the presentation by ancient Israelites of their powerful belligerent neighbours (Egypt, Assyria, Philistines, Babylonians as essentially the incarnations of evil itself and which images have been transmitted in Biblical evangelism till date to the extent that it has inspired the very basis of current dichotomies in similar political representations.

official and informal, spontaneous structures and where each type influences the other in a two-way process. States will structure the relations between its constituent communities by way of legislation and institutions but at the same time its policies will be influenced by the character of intercommunity relations. However the denominator is that the modern nation-state assumes the responsibility of structuring these relations. This is not to relapse into the normative frame of assessing whether such a role is played or not (and how well it is if it is) as others are wont to do. In practice there are variations in terms of efficacy and response to policy at societal level. The history (genealogy) of the classical modern nation-state has been a tragedy in this respect. In one case, it is the cultural genocide which accompanied the brutal institution of uniform languages and cultures in the name of building single nations out of a motley of self-asserting peoples as in the case of the European nations (France, Spain). In another case, it is the problematic attempt by the central aristocracy of one people asserting itself over confederate structures over which it imposes its language and cultural practices (the Hapsburg hegemony in the so-called Holy Roman Empire and later on, Austria-Hungary, English hegemony over the peoples of the British Isles). Yet in others, it was the brutal elimination or subjugation of entire peoples and civilizations to expand the territorial dimensions of the emerged national formations in Europe as Empire building in the Americas and Australia.

One can also note a cyclical movement from fraternity-inspiring universalistic ideals to conflicting trends by a nucleus of some peoples to confrontation with other peoples considered as diametrically opposed and defined as falling outside the sphere of the fraternity. Christendom emerged as a fraternity based universalistic movement based on faith in the ideals and embracing a variety of peoples in Western Europe within its dominion but soon came into a headlong confrontation with an Islamic Umma which itself had brought together a diversity of peoples extending from North Africa right to present-day Iraq. Such a confrontation took on itself the character of the first global war and, in the process, a doctrine initially restricted to a small community of people gained in ascendancy by transforming itself into a principle of political organization and enlarging its borders to the widest possible extent. This cycle finds resistance when the very political hegemony into which this fraternity had grown becomes an alienating principle by working exclusively in the interest of political organization. This is the case of the centrifugal tendency of the nationalities within the so-called Holy Roman

Empire based on papal ascendancy and proclaimed combination of religious subjection and supposed fraternity of peoples both before and in the wake of the Reformation. The nationalities, which were born of resistance to the hegemony to Rome and claimed to organize on the basis of inward looking fraternities within much restricted territory, also sought later to expand their political spaces in logics of confrontation via a hegemonic drive. These are paradoxical drives but they make up the substance of the complexity of historical evolution. New alliances have even emerged in more recent history only to confront other peoples as diametrically opposed that need to be restructured in the image of the perceiving peoples (witness the ill-fated colonial alibi of missions of civilization or white man's burden, the Manichean idea of Evil Empires, axes of evil or clashes of civilizations).

The resultant general historical movement is that of contrasting drives between expansionism in the name of universalism and centrifugal pulls of resistance in particularistic directions by independence movements that prefer to thrive on more localized mixes of arrangements (some complementary, some harmonious, some conflicting). Sooner or later, movements which were movements away from universalising expansion provoke resistance in particularistic directions (see figure 2 below). As such, each national resistance which also seeks to impose an internal process of universalization (through lopsided uniform practices) or even an external process of universalization provokes resistances depending on the character of the process. In the case of colonialism, which is a universalization process based on racial ideologies and assumed hierarchies of culture (civilization, progress), resistance is as much based on the right to self-determination (politics) as on the same racial and cultural grounds (assertion of biological and cultural specificity as equally valid).

Figure 2: Cyclic movment of hegemony and resistance in the tension between universalism and particularism

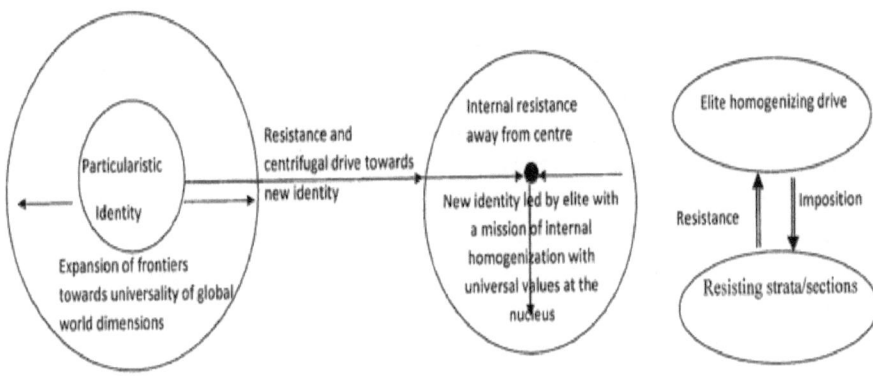

Resistance to universalising trends within the post colonial state, on it part, follows the fault-line of several forms of fragmentation: class and drift towards several forms of vertical differentiation and domination (marginalization, subordination, monopolies of power by a class derived from the independence movement); horizontal differentiation that are grafted to the vertical cleavages (tendency to structure power relations along the lines of the domination of successive tribal elites and exclusion on such grounds); specific identities derived from rather blurred and problematic decolonisation processes that eventually took the character of appendage decolonization (Eritrea into Ethiopia, East Timor into Indonesia, Southern Cameroons into French-speaking Republic of Cameroon, Namibia annexed for some time by Republic of South Africa, Cabinda into Angola, Somaliland into Somalia); and shaky structural arrangements of inequality which survive independence in formerly racially segregated colonies or settlements (USA from the War of Independence and Revolution characterized by formal and instituted segregation until the civil rights movement, post-independence Zimbabwe with its lingering relics of racial segregation, post-apartheid South Africa, the Canadian Union).

Colonial and post colonial interventions have largely structured (in formal terms) and still have structuring effects on certain voluntary and spontaneous relations between peoples within formerly colonized areas of the South. The *Pax colonia* was the declaration of an end to the right of colonized peoples to make war and peace, that is to freely decide to choose between living within communities of conflict, fraternity or accommodation by themselves. In this way it imposed cohabitation within the same space for several peoples some of whom had never been in contact, had only been remotely so or had lived in various forms of intercommunity relations (fraternity, conflict or accommodation). Invariably, each colonial power sought to structure the arrangement of peoples administratively either by redefining peopling in its own warped anthropology or by its own new logic. The new structuring of relations between peoples was largely a colonial definition which was bequeathed to largely anthropologically uninformed people via the selectivity of *évolué* education. In the restructuring frame the oft advanced reasons were cast in conflict models of interpretation of local histories which highlighted overblown histories of migration and conquest. This model of interpretation of intercommunity relations explains the very recourse of competing elites to a tribal mode of competition and the interpretation of every other form of conflict within such a frame. In other words, the colonial and post-colonial regimes imposed an overarching order which streamlined forms of conviviality and reduced every other possible form to one of conflict. The imperative is therefore to replace the old order. That is the illusion of the debate that pits citizen-based and communitarian visions of nation – building and government (democracy). The reality on the contrary points to the regular mixes between the three forms of relations that existed in spontaneous and contingent situations. There are still memories (and commemoration of memories) of fraternity and consensual bonding between peoples, maintenance of relations of animosity (in the absence of the right to engage in warfare) and several forms of accommodation. To these are added new forms of conviviality (intermarriages and friendship ties between peoples of origins far-removed from each other, forms of economic cooperation, competition over political positions) although this takes on more individualistic connotations and forms.

Plural Orders and the Structuring of Relations in the Bicultural Situation

The Anthropology of Structural Relations

While formalization through legislation and institutionalisation has spill over effects, informal relations generated in extra-official contexts (e.g. market situation, extra-curricular interaction between youth, neighbourhood interactions, street gangs, fashion movements in culture) generate emerging trends that may run parallel to, contradict or even give steam to the former. In this way, informal relations may not only be an underside of the social fabric in such a situation but would constitute its very substance. That is why efficacy theorists who invariably conclude by saying that things have not worked as planned get it all wrong. Before looking at efficacy, any viable critique must look at the intrinsic worth of a policy and then question its very basis. What are current in these critiques are assumptions and the treatment of certain trends as givens. For instance, national unity and national integration is taken for granted or as *fait accompli* against the background of which political action is judged. Nobody stops to evaluate both the intrinsic worth and operational value of the concepts. As an effect of the pervading nature of political power these concepts soon gain the force of evidence as they are institutionalised as ordinary social categories of perception. The task of a viable critique is to start by undertaking a critique of the ideological concepts, before proceeding to a critique of the policies deriving thereof. The fundamental flaw with the efficacy approach is that it assumes that if performance were better social conditions will be better. In that regard, it has a value-laden undertone. To the scientist the critique must question the very basis of ideological principles on which practice is built. That is just what we did is the preceding chapters.

An anthropology of conviviality will entail three levels of analysis, namely a level of structure and a level of representations and a level of daily life at macro (national), meso-(community) and micro- (individual) level. At the level of structures one will be concerned with both the structures derived from formal arrangements as well as emerging spontaneous structures. Structured or institutionalised arrangements formalize relations but these formalized arrangements, on their part, have spill over effects (not to use the misleading term, trickle-down effect) into the social fabric as they structure perceptions and representations. Three categories of formal arrangements of the utmost importance stand out at global level. The first of these are the constitutional arrangements that are the result of forced situations and the techniques of *fait accompli*. The evolution of the constitutional process characterized by schemed manipulation has only resulted in controversy and constitutional/legal confusion. The foundations of an expected pluralistic union based on biculturalism and bilingualism which have, over the years, been subverted by undercutting centralization drives initially and subsequently by an open manipulation into a merger through several legal short-cuts with far-reaching effects that range from legalistic opposition from a wide fraction of discontented Anglophone elite through aversion to the state to open calls for secession. It is my opinion that if a referendum were conducted among Anglophone today the results will be much different from President Paul Biya's estimate of 1998 (*Jeune Afrique* No. 1990 2 – 8 March 1998). The malaise may not find its real representation in the separatists (who send shock waves through the regime each time October 1st is approaching) or, worse still, in the few low-key cabinet positions that each government shake-up may confirm or introduce but the general malaise is real. To challenge this observation a referendum can be called as is the case in Quebec or other countries where this is the case.

There is definitely a large undercurrent of popular discontent that needs to be addressed, namely the spill over from the lack of consensus on the formulation of the *fundamental act*. This discontent cannot be compared to the discontent of other disfavoured regions often referred to by Francophone elite. This comparison is based on the equation of the Anglophone community into an ethno-regional entity comparable with others. In such situation, Anglophone claims are drowned in the rather ephemeral and shallow claims of the artificially constructed ethno-regional entities. By the way, Anglophone elite and masses alike can only express their own situation and not that of any other community that is also disfavoured. I have shown that in the 1990s several other constituent factions of elite expressed their own discontent on ethno-regional grounds (Yenshu Vubo 2006:206-7). In any case, the politics of regional balance should have been no cause to such discontent from regions if that was ever the case. The history of roll-back on otherwise performing projects (the federal experiment, the harmonization schemes) in favour of forced orders or techniques of *fait accompli* has only led to a combination of political impasse and the crystallization of difference and differences, at the level of the upper and middle-strata of the society.

Cleavages have also emerged in the direction of an attitude of false comfort and assurance on the part of Francophone elite and general Anglophone resistance, on the one hand, and, on the other, between Anglophone elite associated with government and those excluded from government. The dwindling proportion of Anglophones in positions of government has led to feelings of estrangement where government ministers of Anglophone origin hardly identify with their original Anglophone community. Popular opinions, at best, consider them as "sell-outs" or people who cannot articulate the real interests of their constituencies. Even "home-coming" exercises tend to focus more on the celebration of the *"election by decree"* of the individual by a central government dominated by ethno-regional elite of another region (Yenshu Vubo 2003: 597) than on projecting representation while the slogan of balanced development has been officially phased out from the discourse of government. In the absence of resistance, Anglophones, in the majority, at best, manifest an attitude of indifference, resignation and asymmetrical existence within the polity, this bordering on rejection.

At the more informal level, as I have shown earlier, there are de-structuring effects on population movements within the country and especially the economy in terms of labour, capital, management and entrepreneurship consequent on the dismantling of the federation. These developments have their impact on behavioural attitudes as well as inter- and intra-communal relations. These may be reactions to situations that may have alternatives or may constitute imperatives, aggregations of actions of a spontaneous nature, conflicts or competition or even drifts. An analysis of such a context will point to the development of both specificities and blends: typical Anglophones, typical Francophones; hybrid Anglophones and hybrid Francophones. There are also blends of intercommunity harmony/cooperation, conflicts and accommodation such that nobody with a reductionist view will be right in typifying any situation as totally harmonious (the angelic vision of government ministers), totally a conflict-redden one nor one of only pure accommodation. Harmonious situations translate success stories of the contact, conflicts highlight trouble spots and accommodations point to realism. These will range from economic cooperation between ordinary citizens and neighbourhood relations between families and individuals (children, adults) to relations between people from far-removed areas that find themselves in other areas (either through voluntary migration or imperatives of work) and receiving peoples. Harmony may even be achieved through the constitution of the linguistic communities into separate parallel worlds where each community constructs its communal world separately from the other but with avenues for communication, all in a spirit of respect. This could be considered as a strategy of mutual respect of difference. The mutual understanding between church groups or school children from different cultural streams is a very clear case in point. One can also observe intense interactions and acculturations, which I alluded to when discussing the linguistic question, existing alongside certain forms of low-intensity conflicts over positioning (with its own internal dimension of ethnicity). What is clear is that for now the impending conflagration along dichotomous lines within the polity that has been predicted by several prophets of an apocalypse has not yet taken place.

Anthropology of Representations

Our initial premise was that the polity was cast or generated by and from utopian visions. The fortunes of this union have also been closely associated with this utopian vision. Ordinary perceptions as well as structured representations (ideological writings, slogans, political pronouncements) all hang on this utopian vision: to be with it, without it or to betray it. Utopian visionaries still project the angelic vision by projecting the gains of peace, unity (harmony) and progress (at whatever pace) within the polity while the ordinary people idealise the "other community" when they are faced with problems within their own sub-community within the polity. In the latter respects, it is not uncommon to find Francophone Cameroonians who extol the virtues of Anglophone academics (in the persons of Fonlon, Anomah Ngu, Dorothy Njeuma), school system (witness the current fashion of Francophone elite orientating children into English education at all levels) and systems of government. In fact, the initial massive support for the SDF in the South Western quadrant was derivative of this idealism. If a Francophone system had failed, then the Anglophones who had a better system should be supported to try to lead the country, the argument goes. This was exactly a revival of the utopian visions of the decolonisation period. Conversely, Anglophones elite who are tired of the back-stabbing of their peers usually point to the generally tolerant and accommodating attitude of Francophones. Francophones thus present an angelic alternative to the internal divisions among the elites. Living in French-speaking towns with its opportunities also presents the real glow of city life youngsters of rural origins aspire to. When they can make it this then become ideal models for the rest. A readiness to adopt names from the other linguistic community that has been as old as the union is glaring testimony of this willingness to adopt idealistic visions of the other. This idealism is thus the strong cement of continuing communal life despite the failure of the polity at official levels and would explain the continuing strategies of harmony and accommodation.

Critics of the union highlight its failures and project essentially the cataclysmic and apocalyptic visions of the polity. On the one hand, one finds French-speaking politicians who see no future for the polity as one open for equal participation either on the level of individual citizenship or as constitutional communities. At the heat of political effervescence of the 1990s, some leading Francophone politicians openly described Anglophones as "enemies in the house" or asked them to go elsewhere if they were not satisfied. Some are reported to have echoed the pronouncement by one-time French Interior Minister, Charles Pasqua, that an Anglophone cannot be President of Cameroon. This translates a conception of Anglophones as a community that only has partial status within Cameroon: they could live within Cameroon but not participate on equal terms with other Cameroonians. At the level of more common perceptions the image is that of Anglophones existing only as a subordinate category. Typifications of Anglophones as awkward (Anglo = left handed = not correct = bizarre) and the matching of this typification with denigrating stereotypes are some of the characteristics of this situation. Anglophone reactions have ranged from retort and projections of their own negative stereotypes: the oddity of Francophone manners, a congenital bent towards crookedness and dishonesty in dealings, etc. These perceptions nourish the crystallisation of difference and differences and engender tensions and low- or high- intensity conflicts. The behaviour of politicians acting according to techniques of *fait accompli*, asymmetrical discussions and forced institutionalisation procedures only goes to fuel these perceptions of a heightened sense of difference.

Formal versions of these representations are found in a certain literature that points to an asymmetry in relations. This literature is wide in breadth and constitutes essentially a reaction of the Anglophone intelligentsia to the situation that prevails. One can find these trends in two strands of academic writing: the creative *imaginaire* and its commentators (who also go under the terminology, of critics); social appraisals that may attempt scientific methodologies (but that may or may not be entirely congruent with standard practices which are subverted by their very propensity towards subjectivity).

Prominent portrayals of the union situation in the creative arts (prose, drama, poetry) are found in the creative writings of Bate Besong, Victor Epie Ngome, Nkengasang and the literary criticism of these works by Ambanasom (1996), Bate Besong (1993, 2007), Abety (1996) and Ambe (2007)[32]. While the creative literature is representing and reflecting on the situation of Anglophone Cameroonians, critiques also use the opportunity to highlight the situation often in clearly subjective terms and thus prolonging the essentially propaganda aspect of the politically motivated creative arts. Social science writings inevitably are not spared the subjectivity such that every discussion (book, article) on the national question by Anglophones is on the Anglophone question. The question has become an obsession or opium at worst and an intellectual fashion at its best. Notable among this brand of scholars are Nyamnjoh (1997a, 1997b [with Konings], 2003), Awasom (1998, 2006), Tatah Mentan (1997), Chem-Langhee (1997) and Mbuagbo (2002). Francophone scholars have sort of felt an obligation to exonerate an abstract Francophone community from evident abuses with recourse to equally abstract theories (cf. the works of Nkoum-me–Ntseny and Menthong).

From the strictly bicultural perspective along the English/French divide and its colonial heritage we have a highly plural mix of situations combining symmetrical oppositions based on asymmetrical understandings, utopian drives that sustain the steam of union life and unionism, blends that produce cultural mulattoes and hybrids of the most colourful sorts, accommodations and even separatist dissent which has even inspired separatist tendencies in unsuspecting areas (witness Joseph Owona's reference to Cameroon as a multinational state whose nationalities could go their separate ways if things do not go well and the call by some Beti leaders for a Greater Fang state- utopian in its own way – to include Equatorial Guinea, Cameroon and Gabon). Figure 3 demonstrates this situation very clearly.

---

[32] This is but indicative of trends rather than a comprehensive evaluation which still needs to be done.

Figure 3: Plural Linguistic and Cultural Order resulting from the Situation of Forced Political Order and Multiple Forms of Contact between Speakers of two Received Languages.

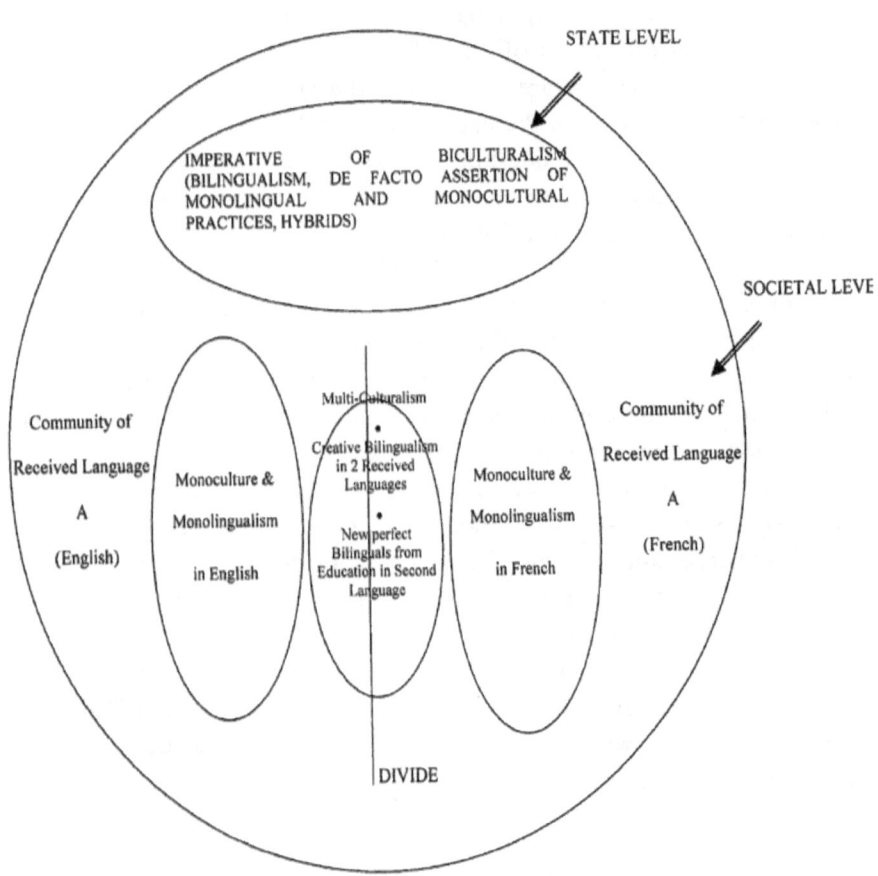

This plural order is complicated further by both an extremely diverse ethno-linguistic situation in real terms and an artificially constructed ethno-regional geopolitical map of the country that is source of its own complex ethnicity question. In such equations the situation variable of *identity* even generates ambiguous categories such as what is called the Eleventh Province that became fashionable when identification with a *Province of Origin* became an important identity label. This category refers to persons or descendants of persons who moved into the British administered sphere especially in the South West Province and who have adopted an English culture but who, now, get caught in the web of political identifications which underlie political aspirations in the post-1990 Biya era. Where are they to identify with? The dilemma is that they cannot identify with their "ethnic origins" which are remote both in their psyche due to the passage of time and lack of contact nor can they identify with their present locations where ideologies of autochthony have generated practices of political exclusion. These are functionally English-speaking Cameroonians in reality but are denied the status of Anglophones defined as indigenes of the former Southern Cameroons, thus in purely historical and geopolitical terms. As the flux of population movements and the history of co-habitation continue in the towns many more of such identities will be generated not only in the current areas but also in the cosmopolitan and metropolitan areas irrespective of the short-lived interludes of autochthony discourses and ideologies.

Current Problems with the Reference to a Colonial Heritage

There are problems with the constant reference to a colonial heritage which has become both an official policy and the alibi not to act in founding a new society after decolonization-unification was effected in the way it was. In fact, there has been no collective examination of the state as a way of providing it with a rational, legitimate and autonomous base. By referring to the heritage of colonialism as the sole basis of founding its plural composition (received laws/bi-jural legal system, bilingualism, biculturalism), the elites of the successive regimes miss the chance of creating a genuinely independent state.

In this regard, the idea of received law is restricted to what was applicable in the colonies during the transitions into statehood (Southern Cameroons, "indigénat") and not the law of the metropolis per se. Benot (op. cit.: 24) is incisive in this regard: "l'appareil d'Etat colonial, tant civil que militaire, obéit à une toute autre logique". It is common knowledge that colonial rule was based on a dichotomy between citizens and subjects, this having repercussions at the level of administration and law. What then does legacy consist of: a copy of the law or education applicable to citizens of the metropolis or that applicable to colonial subjects? If copied from the metropolis or what was applicable to citizens how would this answer the specification of the new state? The idealized liberties and the good produced by the Indirect Rule procedures in the English speaking territories have rather reflected the post-1945 situation with its preparation for handing over. Indirect rule had been decided upon as early as the 1920s in almost all colonial administrations but as a form of self-government it was continually experimented with until the late 1940s with a last reform in the model in the British Cameroons territories. This is the idealized model and not all of indirect rule which was always combined with various forms of direct rule by all colonial regimes (Amselle 1990: 239; Mamdani [2001]19-28). In fact, Mamdani (ibid: 25) has shown that every colonial power eventually made "a shift from direct to indirect rule". This shift was formally sanctioned in the French territories with the Loi Deferre of 1957 (Rivière 2000: 133). It is no wonder that it coincides with reforms that bring about a new legal regime for the territories of Southern Nigeria and Southern Cameroons when the gained quasi-autonomous status by 1955. This regime cannot adopt the status of a gospel given for ever.

In the same way, the perceived brutality and arbitrariness of a Francophone administration as reminiscent of French administrative practices (as perceived by Anglophones) is a real distortion. It is not part of any historically received tradition. These practices were elaborated within the general context of French reluctance to decolonize or decolonize within the context of the famous French Union (cf. Yves Benot op. cit.). In the specific case of French Cameroons such practices were inaugurated in the post-1945 period as the native policy of "indigénat" but, later on, intensified with the radicalization of the nationalist movement. The immediate post-independence period saw a prolongation of a repressive apparatus by the local government, by then only nominally independent. These practices were combined with a wholesale transposition of new juridical–administrative and political practices elaborated under the fourth French Republic that had developed under very peculiar circumstances to give a curious mix of authoritarian rule. This is where we do not only have an over-bearing Executive that dwarfs the other institutions (the Legislative and Judiciary) which are indeed dependent on the former. Repression, arbitrariness and authoritarian rule derive more specifically from the regime of absolute powers ("pleins pouvoirs"), a curious copying from Gaullism that had developed under its own peculiar circumstances, and emergency laws that were meant to prop the new but fragile regime to the exclusion of competing forces with alternative visions such as the UPC.

The corresponding arrangement with the reunification project was to equally transpose and replicate, in fact invent an Anglophone culture/tradition where none had existed prior to 1960. A school system had to be inaugurated by Anglophone elites who had been trained predominantly in Nigerian schools in the colonial era. In the legal domain a whole structure and set of procedures had to be invented within the federated state of West Cameroon. The constitutional guarantees that protected these measures as gains of the union project were to institutionalize claims of a separate culture that would survive well beyond the 1972 act of administrative centralization that abolished the federal experiment. That is why the Anglophone Cameroonian is a complex mix of an English education promoted since independence but also a person integrated into a multicultural Cameroon dominated by French practices. A sustained claim to difference has only been possible by a reproduction of the instrument of that identification which is the school system. However, before the recent appropriation of the Anglo-American higher education model (also styled Anglo-Saxon) in Buea and Bamenda, this claim to autonomy was dwarfed by a predominantly French-speaking university system. The new developments go to provide the new space for the completion of the invention and sustenance of this difference which ensures autonomy and acts as a bulwark against cultural assimilation. The claim to a colonial legacy thus serves to paradoxically guarantee independence only as a 'self-colonization' process (cf. Latouche's [1989] 2005: 94). This may be so only for a moment because it stifles any genuine independence project which is supposed to be a radical creative rupture with the colonial order.

The other limits are contained in the logical formulation of the idea itself. It is not a lineal process transferring good from master to subject but a mix of good and bad habits some uncritically transposed from one context to the other. It ends up inhibiting the entire process of rupture with the colonial order to invent a new one. The idea of legacy itself is even logically incompatible with the claim to independence. With the Francophones it has facilitated and combined neocolonialism with cultural assimilation and ended up subverting the very idea of autonomy. In the English-speaking Cameroonian it has been idealizing what was never lived in the 55 years of mandate rule and appropriated it as the only way out thus implying a certain nostalgia for a past that never existed. The idea of colonial legacy is the refusal to be independent, which in essence is the claim to the status of an autonomous subject with the capacity of a self-conscious agent, one who makes his/her own history.

One of the negative outcomes of this situation is the crystallization of a dichotomy that has degenerated into a conflict: first as an open confrontation between cultures presented as incompatible; second as a political conflict between elites (taken globally as Anglophone or Francophone) over the control of and ascendancy within the state apparatus; lastly, as a competition between formal systems (educational systems, legal system) for ascendancy. The first consequence is that this renders formal communication, dialogue and cohabitation/accommodation difficult. This is what explains the feeling among Anglophones that they are discriminated against by a callous Francophone majority. Conversely, this is at the background of hostility from some Francophone elite who feel that the Anglophone presence is an intrusion and even unwelcome[33]. The poplar imagery is of strange bedfellows as captured in Epie's Ngome's un-natural marriage, "what God has put asunder". The second consequence is that Francophone elite in power wish to maintain a dominant position within the state apparatus in global terms even if there is a drive towards ethno-regional arrangements (northerner, Bamileke, Sawa, Beti).

Even when there is a feigned idea of balance, Anglophones are not treated as a constitutional component. They are reduced to an invented ethno-regional entity as they are awarded the same status as the northerners, Beti and Bamileke[34]. As such times their claims as a specific community are down-played as they are compared with other newly invented categories that are invented for the purpose. If they ask to be treated as a constitutional minority on the basis of their specific modern culture against that of a

---

[33] This tendency had been observed far back in the days before the reunification when an official in the British colonial office had observed that "some people in French Cameroon do not really want the Southern Cameroons to join them whatever they have said in public" (Ngoh 2011: 45).

[34] Witness this newspaper caption: "Paul Biya préfère les Anglophones aux Sawa" (*Aurore Plus No.* 1278, 10 December 2010). This is very telling since it was the very concept of Sawa which was used in the 1990s to undercut the restive and buoyant All Anglophone Conference movement, a strategy that succeeded so well as to reduce that movement to competing clandestine voices with no real force. This caption is even misleading as it does not reflect the article itself. The president had decided to spend an extra night in Douala during his 2010 visit to Bamenda. This is to raise the trivial to the status of the sublime. One thing is certain: to the writer's eye the Anglophone category always has to be pitted against that of Sawa or autochthones. This seems to be an officious dimension of the attitudes dominant elites which is betrayed by an unsuspecting journalist.

French-speaking majority, this claim is subverted with the category of indigenous minority that is easily given constitutional status with no struggle (see clauses on the protection of minorities in 1996 Amendment; Konings and Nyamnjoh 2000). Progressively, as one ethno-regional entity obtains near complete hegemony over the state apparatus (in the majority of senior positions), anything that claims to be Anglophone is reduced to a disproportionately, incongruous, insignificant and token presence in government and administration.

The worst scenario is when the Anglophone community is lumped together with the Bamileke as the newly invented category of the Anglo-Bami (following the emergence of the SDF) and is vilified, physically molested in several parts of the country and openly discriminated against. The elites are later on emasculated and reduced paradoxically to clowning apologists of the system that excludes them or used to obstruct the articulation of the interests of this community. For instance, the few Anglophone elites in government are those who are not only the most violent critics of the autonomist movement, the SCNC; they are the most active campaigners against this movement. They, obviously, do not have any other message than that the system has no problem.

The competition for ascendancy between the formal modern systems has borne with it the looming spectre of assimilation that Anglophones have feared over generations. At every juncture some element of the Anglophone community have had to actively oppose attempts either at dwarfing what they consider the essence of an educational system that has to be their own (witness the GCE syllabus crisis of 1983, the struggle for the GCE Board, the campaign for the "Anglo-Saxon" University of Buea in the early 1990s, struggle over conditions of promotion in the universities) before they could have it their own way. In fact, there is a certain struggle to assert the primacy of the French system of measures as against the English some Francophone elites taking the lead in this regard. In the educational sphere there is an overt attempt at higher education to both accept the necessity of difference while proving that the better system is the French all this in the name of integration. In each situation the Francophone elites do not find anything wrong with a system where education should be aligned to that of the dominantly French speaking population. In the spirit of conquest, the General Certificate of Education could be organized in the same way as the Baccalauréat as with the group certificate project of 1983. It looks as if there is nothing wrong with a technical education organized and taught by staff that do not understand the language of the students (as in the days of the Anglophone *Baccalauréat Technique*) or Anglophone students continue to study at university level in a French language that they do not master. Attempts to correct the abuses of such historical development are treated as a travesty of the normal[35]. That is why the Francophone elites consider any Anglophone claim as a "surenchère" (putting the stakes very high). If such measures that tend to dominate Anglophones succeed then the fear of assimilation that haunts Anglophones will become a reality. When the elites find nothing wrong then the controllers of the system drive home the point and can then act with impunity. As the terrain has shifted from that of cohabitation to an imbalanced struggle between unequal forces (because power is de facto in the hands of Francophone elites), this has given way to an increasing deconstruction of Anglophones as a people hoping to organize itself into a system. In this frame of things, national unity or bilingualism means that Anglophones should understand and speak two languages while Francophones may not.

Some of the strategic gains that Anglophone founding fathers made during the early years of the union have been eroded. There is also a widening gap between Anglophone pro-regime elites, on the one hand, and the excluded elites, masses in the rural areas and areas farther away from the important urban centers of Bamenda, Limbe, Buea, and Kumba, on the other. There is an increasing tendency for Anglophones not to count as an important voice in the polity except either as uncritical acquiescing voices, underground activists with no following worth the name or a silent passive

---

[35] Franck Essomba of *Le Messager* Newspaper finds the creation of the University of Bamenda in the Anglo-American tradition to be anti-constitutional and a way of destroying "national integration": "Université de Bamenda: Paul Biya attente à l'intégration nationale", reads the caption of an article of edition No. 3303 of 11 March 2011. He continues in the article to assert in the sub-title that: "En créant les universités anglo-saxonnes uniquement dans l'ancien Southern Cameroons, le chef de l'Etat renforce le repli linguistique et culturel, bat en brèche le principe d'intégration nationale…consigné dans la constitution du 18 janvier 1996…le gouvernement …vient de jeter apparemment les bases d'une partition profonde de l'Etat camerounais…elle risque de déboucher [sur] une 'conscience anglophone' tournée vers le sectarisme et le rejet de l'autre ». The underlying assumption is Anglophone claims can only be negative and if met they will only lead to disastrous consequences for the country. This cannot be taken as an isolated statement because the Buea experiment has not led to the outcomes that the journalist foresees for Bamenda which is not exclusively for "the natives of the former Southern Cameroons" as he claims. He is only motivated by the stereotypes among some Francophones that Anglophones are separatists and that the request for autonomy is synonymous with secession. These are the extremist positions that make Anglophones uncomfortable.

but grumbling majority. The debate on cohabitation or communality seems to be closed with a foregone conclusion, namely that it will never be opened again. In that situation the Anglophone community seems to be trapped in a fix and at dangerous cross-roads.

Towards a Politics of Possibilities

Such complicated situations place enormous responsibilities on the Cameroon polity in terms of redressing a fractured situation that has resulted from the history and generation of the plural order in terms of form, representations and practices. The politics of *fait accompli* or *forced political engineering* resulting in the slogan of the nation of Cameroon being "one and indivisible"[36] has proved to be nothing but wishful thinking because of the lack of the means to effect it. This is even an empty slogan carried over from the Gaullist France among many other things. In reality it has survived as a reflex, the kind Bourdieu calls "automatisme verbal". To come back to a quote I have made before:

> Les nations ne sont pas unes et indivisibles (unique and fixed). A travers l'histoire, il est possible de relever la désintégration de quelques nations qui jouèrent pourtant un rôle important durant une période particulière de même qu'il est possible de repérer la création de nouvelles nations. [Nations are not one and indivisible. Throughout history it is possible to identify the disintegration of certain nations that have played important roles at given epochs as it is possible to identify the creation of new nations.] Guibernau (2003: 284) (*Translation mine*)

In this particular case before us the nation-state is a staggering project towards a oneness but whose unity exists only in its territorial dimensions. The reality, on the contrary is a problematic plurality that calls for solutions. In the search for solutions there is a need for a veritable revolution that will have to change both attitudes and structures. Each of the three essential components of a critical analysis (politics, culture and society) can only be better addressed both individually and in relation to each other in an integrated and systemic manner.

---

[36] This sounds curiously like the call for rallying to the "La République française une et indivisible" (Benot op. cit.: 88).

Politically, there is an imperative for a re-opening of the debate on the form of the state. Firstly, this is necessitated by the current crises of unity that must be solved. There is an imperative for a re-opening of the debate on the form of the state as is necessitated by the current crises of unity. No one has and would ever have a logical right to close the debate on the form of the state given the way the constitutional political engineering has taken place. Nobody can lock up the destiny of any group of people and how they have to live together through manipulation in the name of intellectual legitimacy (often claimed by constitutional law scholars). It is common knowledge that Sengat Kuo was the most prominent invisible hand that crafted the 1972 constitution suspending the Federal Constitution which Ahidjo got voted in ignorance and in a climate of terror. That was the highest proof of intellectual dictatorship used to hoodwink an unsuspecting Cameroonian people.

The 1996 overhaul, which could have been the enactment of a totally new one, was played between the legal luminaries of Yaoundé II (SOA) within the Technical drafting committee - namely a Francophone bench and an Anglophone one – wherein the battle was not that of ideas and negotiations between stakeholders. It was rather a process of cooptation wherein the Executive had its own experts to rationalise positions that were already adopted by the regime. In this way, the lively debates that had preceded the process and had occasioned it were shelved aside and the promised nation-wide debate that was to ensure that all shades of opinion were taken into consideration simply never took place. As it turned out, there were serious cleavages within that committee, first along the linguistic divide which saw the sidelining of the Anglophone group and then among the Francophone professors who had hijacked the process itself. The linguistic split created the All Anglophone Conferences that later degenerated into the separatist factions that are the central question in the union. History will register it that it was the intransigence of the Francophone component of this Committee that created the crisis of separatism by not giving a voice to the Anglophones through this constitutional debate. The doctrinal differences between the professors (cf. Nguini 1998: 51) who were still in the Committee were settled by privileged relations with the President rather than salient arguments. That is why the draft of the president of that committee won the day as constitution over drafts that had been presented by the Anglophone team and the two other Francophone professors. This explains the selective attitude to issues of the day: operate within the narrow definition of minorities to refer to local peoples facing pressure from urbanisation (labelled autochthonous or indigenous minorities) as against the distinctive linguistic and political minority status of Anglophones; give the semblance of change by announcing reforms while remaining fundamentally conservative (creating democratic institutions and suspending their application by clauses of progressive application; arranging the constitution to suit the President; reinforcing the powers of the Executive as against other arms of the government in the name of a false doctrine of "governing democracy").

With the Anglophone component out of the way the unitary state was reaffirmed in a wonderful oxymoron or double speak by declaring it decentralised "Etat unitaire decentralisé", it would be itself as unitary (this meaning centralized) but be at the same time decentralised, itself and its opposite. This was in direct lineal genealogy to the centralized federation that has always been a dream to the founders of the polity since Ahidjo. No reference was made to Anglophone federalist claims (whether in two or several units), federalism having been declared anathema and inimical to a form of unity arbitrarily decided by the all-knowing pundits of the system[37]. This was all in a logic in which the regime had set out to weed out any concessions or constitutional guarantees to the Anglophones in the Ahidjo years as in the way it had dismantled the policy of regional balance. Little wonder that it was the same person who was at the basis of the new regressive changes were taking place. At an earlier period as Minister of the Public Service and Administrative Reforms he had annulled the policy of regional balance by arguing that all citizens had to be placed on the same footing in competitive examinations into the public service rather than according to a quota system in which each province was represented as in the past[38]. As the earlier reform had opened the way for the creation of a hegemonic position for the elites of the Centre and South provinces in all spheres of public life (through discretional appointments and favouritism in recruitments), the new minorities created by the new constitution in an objective alliance (Beti in Yaoundé, Sawa in the Littoral) have emerged into a protected and dominant position.

---

[37] It only remains to be declared illegal or treasonable.
[38] Curiously, this has become an issue of public concern even from the regime itself. Witness the crisis surrounding the entrance examination into the Faculty of Health Sciences at the University of Buea in 2006 when the Ministry of Higher was arguing for regional balance.

The choice of a parliamentary mode for adopting the constitutional revisions avoided the possibility of a rejection form a people still being in the main opposed to the regime. The personal interests of the drafters would prevail but that would not stop its short comings from being exposed as are the present criticisms of the constitution form eminent scholars. Even the sustained campaigns from activists has not forced the regime to reconsider view its position. On the contrary, Anglophone elites in government have been exclusively requisitioned at the forefront of a campaign against separatism without proposing alternatives. What was at work was intellectual dictatorship coupled with callousness from the elites of a linguistic majority. Such processes only end up distancing societies from their governing classes when society-wide issues are transformed into debates between isolated elites, in this case self-appointed all-knowing intellectuals at the service of the Prince. The latter category thus substitutes the domination of foreign advisers through a sectional appropriation which establishes new relations of domination and alienation and exclusion that can be likened to internal colonialism. What can be observed here are multiple cleavages, between elites and masses and between elites of the region that holds power[39] and the others which stand in a relationship of internal colonialism by virtue of the fact that one region has a sweeping sway over public management. This process sanctions the legal expertise of Yaoundé II as the new but concealed theatre for constitutional engineering as well as its Francophone pontiffs as the source of legitimacy, doctrine and dogma[40] as opposed to the exclusion of Anglophones whose contributions would have enriched the fundamental law in the spirit of the promised blending or harmonisation of cultures at the basis of the union.

Parliamentary voting, which pays attention only to the final "majority vote" over national issues and where concerned people cannot have a proportionately important say in matters of exclusive concern to them (as is the case with Anglophones) or where only the opinions of those authorised to express favourable opinions are respected, is a dictatorship and infringes on the fundamental democratic principle of adopting majority sway while respecting minority opinion. An institutional framework, which excludes extra-institutional debates on national issues, is a dictatorship. The most

---

[39] Witness the telling metaphor of "pays organisateur", to cynically mean the tribe in control, used to refer to the Beti-Fang-Bulu country.
[40] Even the debates about the flaws of the 1996 revision prior to the 2011 elections were concentrated around Yaoundé II.

democratic option to open up the debate and involve all because no debates are closed forever, nor are there people who are mandated to speak on behalf of people for ever. This is consistent with Ernest Renan's famous dictum to the effect that a nation is a daily plebiscite ("La nation est un plebisicite de tous les jours"/The nation is a plebiscite that takes place everyday). Any claims to solutions found once and for all are proof of totalitarianism.

At the level of institutions, there must be a readiness to discuss all historically viable options: one nation – two cultures option (federalism, two school systems, two judicial systems); harmonization; blends of harmonization and one nation-two cultures option. Presently there are only assumptions about which over-all principle operates and, these, as situations arise. The institutional framework is therefore at best erratic. This is reflected in the assumptions of citizens and their reactions to the state. There should be a critical rethinking of the institutional basis of the state and it would be irresponsible not to do so. To claim that this exists as a foregone conclusion is to be dishonest and to fail to be responsive to the general interest. It is the general institutional basis that gives coherence to institutional practices, the responses to these policies and the much needed harmony at societal level. Distorted and contradictory practices are the result of a void borne of techniques of *fait accompli* and claims of foregone conclusions. In exploring solutions, lessons can be learnt from countries with a comparable situation to that of Cameroon. Examples are the constitutional arrangements within Spain (that accommodate its Catalonian and Basque components), Canada (with its French-speaking minority) or Switzerland (with its four linguistic communities and its cantons). Cameroon is not an island that can hope to invent so original a model.

At the level of ordering and structuring social relations a balance sheet of national unity and integration schemes (resettlement schemes, incitation to settle anywhere in the country, equality of citizenship, protection of minority cultures – not the warped concept of indigenous minority-, regional balance) should be undertaken (much further than this work has done) and furthered. It was irresponsible for the Biya regime to have fed autochthony discourses and profiteered from the autochthony movement of the so-called Sawa and to have enshrined autochthony clauses in the constitution. The fundamental problem of geographical imbalance in growth poles in favour of Douala and Yaoundé in particular, and the coastal areas in general need to be addressed by balancing growth poles further inland. Points of harmonious integration and accommodation should be used as entry points for further integration and conviviality. In this process while there is a search for solutions to conflicts, tensions and contradictions, the existence of colourful creative possibilities should be pointers to the search for openings to such possibilities in accommodation, cosmopolitanism, accommodation and cooperation. It is even this level of analysis that should be the focal point of the construction of a new polity. Again the unilateral abolition of equilibrium solutions without a national debate on the question (evidently pushed by tribal motives) can only be interpreted as an anti-democratic imposition.

There is a subscription to superficial regional integration projects with no viability and the transfer to that level or the substitution of real internal debates over issues of importance with trivial international agenda contributing to the distancing of the state from society. Can national integration (not to be confused with the abusive corruption of the term by the Biya regime) be substituted with regional integration understood in the very narrow sense of greater affiliation with the countries of the former Afrique Equatoriale française (AEF)? Can the Anglophone problem be eclipsed in favour of preoccupation with CEMAC? These are the essential questions the regime is eluding and the emblematic choices it has to make. How can Cameroon take on the additional and problematic burden of regional integration when it has not yet resolved its own crisis of integration? Is it not hypocritical to subscribe to sub-regional integration projects when the regime is manipulating social cleavages for political ends? Witness the invention of autochthony and the mobilization against non-natives referred to as settlers, "strangers" within the period of political liberalization by the regime. Why must Cameroon invest so much in such an unworkable or poorly performing project (it is least integrated in Africa), when there are other priorities? Why should such projects also work against segments of the population that are not contiguous to other countries of CEMAC? Cameroon has not taken English to the CEMAC which seems to the affair of Francophones that essentially excludes Anglophones. If it is multilingual as it incorporates Spanish (for Equatorial Guinea) and Portuguese (for Sao Tome e Principe), it is mute about the English language. French is taken for granted as the dominant language and nothing is said about the bilingual nature of the country.

Cameroon's international status as a Francophone country is affirmed and asserted in an undeclared manner. There is an evident need to revisit foreign policy options that oblige Cameroon to compromise the exigencies of the bicultural situation. Although some English speaking African countries are exploring ways of benefiting from the harmonization of some transnational legislation it is not a reason for the Cameroon state to engage itself in conventions that would run contrary to internal policy and practices. Indeed, there needs to be congruence between foreign and internal policies and practices. The bicultural/multicultural status of Cameroon must be clearly projected in foreign policy and not only simply brandished as an internal policy ploy to which only lip service is occasionally paid or as fashionable foreign policy gimmicks. The current instinctive drift to follow in the line of sub-regionalisation schemes that follow in the strict colonial history is not only proof of imbalance and myopia but also insensitivity to the obligations that an internal situation places on foreign policy which itself impacts on local policy concerns. It is also an unrealistic bid where Cameroon almost has no gains to make even in terms of regional hegemony. Cameroon should also explore foreign policy options in more realistic directions such as a rapprochement or even eventual integration into a West African Union (ECOWAS[41]) with whom Cameroon has much more affinity and as a movement from a more problematic "neo-AEF" scheme taken as an automatic option. A reorientation can be viable within the scope of a sustained public discussion between stake holders and should not be the monopoly of bureaucratic elites whose unilateral definition of foreign policy orientations is only tantamount to dictatorship of the intelligentsia and anti-democratic practice.

As a way foreword the debate on conviviality and thus the relations between the cultures, the formal modern systems and within the polity needs to be re-opened and made to transcend the binary vision based on competition/conflict. It needs to be also based on tolerance, readiness to learn and a readiness to take the best of each other system. It must also be ready to go beyond the colonial frame or vision which has imprisoned the outlook of the ruling class. It will have to learn from the past (to improve on it), reason from current exigencies (to solve real problems) and project into the future (to target more enduring solutions for coming generations). In this way, such a process is rooted in the search for solutions to the very essence of the problems themselves while reading the best of a past that offered its solutions (the past then is a form of capital understood as accumulated value). The solutions to the crisis of this bicultural situation will also be

---

[41] Cameroon had an observer status within this organization but it is not clear why it is no more so.

situated within the general context of cultural diversity with its own crisis (Yenshu Vubo 2011).

Revisiting the Constitution

The following proposals that I have made before can serve as a starting point.

In the opinion page of *The Post* of Monday January 14th 2008, I made a critique of president Biya's speech on New Year Eve 2008. In that article I was fundamentally opposed to the partisan and piecemeal nature of the constitutional revisions that were currently being clamored for by the president and the CPDM. I would wish to come back to elaborate on the different amendments I proposed and the form any revisions may take. The aim here is to explain to the public why I take exception to some of the articles and why they need to be modified or weeded out of the present fundamental law.

Revision of Article I: The name of the country

The change of the name of the country from that of "United Republic" to "Republic" in short has been the source of disenchantment for Anglophone Cameroonians who have read into it the culmination of a long-term strategy of assimilation. If the token reminder of a process of unification is implied in the term "United," its elimination in the way it was done (by parliamentary amendment when it was voted by referendum) is logically argued to either imply annexation of the other component of the polity (ex-Southern Cameroons) or withdrawal to the status quo of 1960-1961 by the former independent French-speaking Republic of Cameroon. Some people may ask: what is in a name? That is the very heart of symbolic attachment to a polity. That the former British colonies of North America took independence as the "United States" or that the kingdom of Great Britain is "United" is as important as to whether Cameroon is "United". We cannot preach unity so much and be oblivious of the very fact of our being "United" in our own very name. It is the much about our history that we cannot forget.

Revision of Article 1.2: The Form of the State

It is pure hypocrisy to continue assisting on the unitary and Jacobin model when it is common knowledge that it has failed. The most appropriate form of a state organization for a multicultural nation like Cameroon is a federation along the lines of its plural and diverse nature. I am aware of the fact that the very idea of a federation sends shock waves through some people (especially the French speaking elite). There need to be no fear because the majority of Cameroonians are fundamentally regional federalists who have a strong sense of attachment to their areas. For now, the federal option would best serve the interest of linguistic and cultural diversity. Several forms of this federalism have been proposed (taking the linguistic division inherited at reunification as basic starting point) and it would take only a sustained debate within a constitutional conference to arrive at a suitable form for the moment.

The federal model of modern states has arisen out of arrangements which lumped historically and culturally distinct but strong peoples together. This is the case of the Belgian experience which brings together the Flemish, French and Germans and the Swiss experience which associates French, German and Italian elements. One can also include in this category the experience of Luxembourg with its German and French elements. These communities have maintained their cultural pluralism only with elaborate social contracts wherein the historic communities have obligations of respect for each other. They have thus become the model for other modern nation-state structures although they were the exception rather than the rule. Llobera (1994) argues that although federations "were not the preferred model of the early modern periods ... they have a strong appeal ... [as] many a nation turns out to be a multinational state on close inspection".

In practical terms the decentralization achieved within the scope of a federalist tendency has led to enormous progress in the solution of intercommunity tensions or laying to rest so-called irredentist tendencies. In this regard, de Rohan (2003: 13) surmises that:

La Belgique n'a pu subsister qu'au prix d'une reforme constitutionnelle qui instaurait un fédéralisme très élaboré, fondé sur un équilibre rigoureux entre les trois communautés linguistiques, flamand, Francophone et germanique.

Seul l'avènement en Espagne d'un régime démocratique a permis aux Basques et aux Catalans de bénéficier d'une très large autonomie reconnaissant leur spécificité. Les autonomies italiennes n'ont pu se développer qu'à l'intérieur d'un cadre constitutionnel nouveau au lendemain de la dissolution du fascisme./Belgium only survived thanks to a constitutional reform which instituted a well elaborated federalism based on a rigorous equilibrium between the three Flemish, French and German linguistic communities.

Only the advent of a democratic regime in Spain enabled the Basque and Catalonians to benefit from an autonomy that recognized their specific status. Autonomous entities in Italy could only develop within a new constitutional dispensation in the aftermath of the evacuation of fascism.

For Guibernau (op. cit.: 281) the argument is the management of diversity:

> Un Etat multinational reconnait explicitement sa diversité interne et, par là même, pèse sur les diverses définitions du nationalisme qui peuvent émerger sur son territoire. Dans un tel cas, le nationalisme induit par l'Etat impliquera, tout d'abord, nécessairement, l'acceptation des différentes nations vivant à l'intérieur de ses frontières. /A multinational state openly recognizes its internal diversity and, through that, can influence the various connotations that nationalism can take within its territorial confines. In such a case, nationalism that is initiated by the state will, as a precondition and of necessity, mean that the different nations living within its borders.

Savidan (2003: 247) argues that the stakes of this process have been principally development and the enhancement of democracy.

L'enjeu de la décentralisation bien entendue est sans doute d'améliorer les services publics offerts à la population concernée, mais il est ausside restituer localement des espaces de déliberation, dans le cadre desquels le pouvoir politique des élus puisse être directement engagé./The challenge of decentralization, of course, is without doubt, to improve the public services of the people concerned, but also to restore the spaces of discussion at local level so that the political powers of elected persons can be directly taken to task. (*Translation mine*)

If the nation-state building project suffers stagnation because of the essentially coercive nature of the project, we can only propose the contrary namely that it will work if it is undertaken in a spirit of tolerance, complementary relations and cooperation between the plural cultures that characterize it. This implies that we have to abandon the modernist premise that the unity of the nation-in-the- making can only be achieved through the 'creative destruction" of pre-existing cultures or their necessary transcendence as postulated by politicians (Biya 1987:120; Nyerere 1966: 171) in the image of a supra-ethnic cultural project (Morin 1994: 166). What I mean is that the will to live together, which should characterize a national consciousness, is still predicated on a dialectics of superimposition- exclusion in the image of a society without an alternative project. The answer to the question whether one can achieve national cohesion in a context of cultural pluralism is that it is possible because this was possible between local historic communities and because this has been possible within some modern state structures. This has been possible largely due to some strategies that can serve as lessons to policy makers in the modern context.

One should be careful of one-dimensional visions that consider the present nation-state in its present form as the only model on which societies have to be organized. Three scientific observations dictate the path that can be taken. Firstly, one needs to take note of the specificity of the nation-state. In other words one has to take the nation-state as "…an historical product, one which is localized in time and space" (Amin 1998: 57) that cannot be transposed wholesale or generalized abusively. Secondly, the historical process by which this was possible is situated at the longue durée (Llobera op. cit.). Idealized visions of the nation-state stress its unique and its indivisible character as is often the case of sloganeering in Cameroon.

One therefore has to take into account the fact that peripheral states are lacking in historical depth and as I have indicated elsewhere "it will take a long time for the formation of the overarching structures of African national identities to be realized" (Yenshu Vubo 2003: 621). Lastly, as Llobera (op. cit.: 220) argues, nations cannot be created *ex nihilo*. This last point argues for the abandonment of utopian models of nation building colonial models of management characterized by repression, coercion and a hegemonic drive whose supreme goal is to obliterate local historical realities perceived as essentially problematic.

Revision of Article 57: Organs of Regional Council

In the federalist spirit of the proposal to revise Article 1.2, the regions should be called provinces as before but have assemblies with legislative powers and regional governments as a way of giving them real autonomy. There is an obsession with the term "region" since the early days of the union when the country was carved out into regions in 1962. Countries such as Canada and South Africa are federations whose decentralized territorial organs are provinces. The change in name does not usher automatically into the autonomy requested.

Elections should be through direct universal suffrage in order to ensure participation and avoid some elections automatically influencing others as is the case with the current constitution. The current legislation in this regard needs to be revisited. The autochthony clause in 57.3 needs to be replaced with one that rather stresses a residency clause in order to avoid situations where, in the name of autochthony, some people get disenfranchised and are obliged to return to their regions of origin to run for elections or vote. It was irresponsible for the regime to have fed on autochthony discourses and profiteered from the autochthony movement of the 1990s and to have enshrined autochthony clauses in the constitution.

Abrogation of Article 58: Government Delegates to Regions

The appointment of government delegates subverts the very idea of autonomy that is at the basis of organs of a decentralized or federalist type. This contradicts the very idea of giving power to the local level: taking with the left hand what has been given with the right. This is also true of local councils whose action has been dwarfed by government delegates and "prefects".

Abrogation and Modification of Article 61

The provinces should not automatically be transformed into regions. The regions should be drawn through a constituent assembly. This is a political issue that cannot be decreed through a constitution or by a head of state alone.

I now return to the rationale for a new constitutional conference to usher in a comprehensive revision. For one thing, the present constitution is not a consensual one. Cameroonians need to be reminded of the fact that the widespread discontent in the Anglophone community is the direct result of two major modifications: that of 1984 which modified the name of the country and that of 1996 whose process obstinately closed the doors on discussions on the constitutional status of the English speaking community. These two revisions have only gone to compound the institutional problems that were initiated at foundation with the inconclusive arrangements and asymmetrical debates of the so-called Foumban conference, the manipulations that ushered in the unitary state in 1992 and the forced political order that has been at work ever since then. The only consensual way of coming out of this situation is to return to a constitutional conference that can arrive at a consensus. The habitual hate slogans proffered by pro-regime Anglophone elites against dissenting voices are no solution at all. Neither will persistent harassment of dissenters who have chosen the extremist position be helpful. It can only add to the protest movement. This is the lesson from sociology:

Refuser l'hypothèse même de la conflictualité, ce n'est pas assurer l'ordre et la paix sociale, c'est plutôt favoriser les conduites de crise, à commencer par celles de la violence/To refuse the possibility of conflict is not an assurance that there will be order or social peace. It will rather promote actions that reflect crises, starting with acts of violence (Wieviorka 2010: 250)

Institutional Reforms

I have called elsewhere for a general reform of the state in Africa as a solution to the problem of ethnic diversity (Vubo 2011) with a call for a movement away from the colonial basis of the state. We have also criticized this state earlier in this work for its persistence in the name of a paradoxical claim to a colonial legacy in a context where independence would have meant a rupture.

This reform we feel will be inscribed as far as Cameroon is concerned in a number of principles such as equality, equity and social justice. Concerning the bicultural situation, there will be a need to talk about the protection of specificities and not minorities that are ill-defined at the present moment. In this regard, the imperative will be to specifically replace the former concept with social policy measures that target specific issues of concern to people with specific social crises. As such, policy should dissociate the approach to social problems from identity claims in order to forestall their manipulation by politicians (Yenshu Vubo 2003: 153). The state of Cameroon has failed in its promise to defend the interests of what was called indigenous minorities as the clause of exclusive rights in their once exclusive ethnic homelands has not worked at all. In the first place, it was a pure myth to make such promises because it is contrary to the logic and reality of urban development in major cities in regions to the South of the country (Bamenda, Bafoussam, Douala, Kumba, Nkonsamba, Yaounde)[42]. These are irreversible realities with different degrees of complexity. Short-lived protection was only possible through a disproportionate appointment of elites from these areas into government positions, the disenfranchisement of non-natives and regression in terms of social integration, generating with it hate and xenophobia. If this dangerous political ideology short-lived secured some form of representation for natives (labeled "indigenous minorities") after the 1996 municipal elections, it was thanks to strategies of electoral exclusion under the ambit of the ruling Cameroon People's Democratic Movement. This is why one can talk of profiteering. Such a situation has collapsed with time so much so that the spectrum of representation has changed completely in the metropolitan areas of Wouri (principally Douala), Mungo, Fako and Mfoundi to reflect their diversity.

The institution of "indigenous" government delegates to control urban agglomerations in these areas has not been helpful to the local peoples because their vocation is not limited to natives. Moreover, their capacity to manage the complexities is just wanting such that their balance sheet is as poor as that of indigenous mayors in cosmopolitan areas. Such drives also run the risk of alienating other stakeholders (non-natives in this regard) who often loss the sense of belonging, participation and ownership. Besides being a source of political apathy and hostility, this simply kills the zeal to participate in the development of these areas. This also sidetracks from the basic issues which are lack of urban planning, absence of social policy (especially affirmative action targeting social problems) and overbearing capitalist expansion from both national and multinational companies. The logic of this constitutional clause is simply flawed and empirically unworkable. It has also lost in appeal and is replaced with partisan messages

---

[42] The reality of composite towns in the three northern provinces is markedly different and would pose different types of problems.

that are also anchored in ethnic jingoism (Duala vs. Bamileke, Beti vs. Bamileke, Sawa vs. Grafi). The paradox is that the same people encouraging such tendencies cohabit in government, are militants of the same political party, live in the same neighbourhoods and cooperate in business. This policy is a failed one while the reality of the problem of urban development is stark and acute. The better alternative could be a *special urbanized peoples' plan* wherein specific affirmative actions will have to be adopted undertaken to redress their problems. This will entail resettlement schemes, low cost housing, education for disadvantaged children, employment, health, etc.

Without taking the risk of repeating myself, I wish to stress the importance of this point because ethnicity has constituted the smokescreen, the veil behind which the social question gets circumvented or is masked, the high ground on which elites perch in the quest for power and the safety or alibi-ideology for competing bourgeois elements lacking in social programmes and policies (Amin op. cit.: 56). One dimension of the problematic of pluralism can therefore be tackled by socially grounded development policies comprehensive enough to tackle the multiple crises that rocks the very basis of the state which the skewed nature and paucity of current policies is unable to handle. These policies should not be imbedded in the fads invented by so-called funding institutions but should derive from a critical evaluation and a realistic deployment of indigenous means. This implies a profound reflection on the concepts of democracy, rights and welfare starting with Amin's radical definition of democracy as the "acceptance of plurality and the recognition of certain core rights" (Amin n. d.; see also Yenshu 1997). For a long time the concept of rights has been restricted in domains of applicability (e.g. the economic domain for which it was excluded for a long time) and the categories of people to whom it was applied. In its social dimension democracy has to give back to people the status of actors and not passive subjects of dominant historical processes against which they can have no conscious alternatives (as is the case with the gospel of globalisation) or objects of manipulation by elites through perverted versions of democracy.

Management of Linguistic Difference

In relation to the linguistic question, there should be a national and well-planned policy for the official languages which is our concern here. For now, the reference to bilingualism is vague and it is left to citizens to decide which option to choose. There should be clear cut domains for the two languages: it should be clearly spelt out where each or both apply. The reality is that the centre has to be bilingual while the two linguistic communities can cohabit in parallel manner in their separate geographical spheres. The vague claim that all Cameroonians can be bilingual and that they should be is simply utopian and impossible. No country in Cameroon's position (Belgium, Switzerland, Canada) has ever pretended to have more than one language spoken by *every* citizen. On the contrary, linguistic specificities have argued for official linguistic difference as in the case of Catalonia with its high degree of autonomy and the use of the Catalans at the regional level. In the spirit of federalism that we are proposing the centre must be completely bilingual and measures taken to ensure that. For example, all civil servants could be obliged to meet requirements of competence in the second language or train in that language to work at central level. This is what could be called obligatory bilingualism which can be contrasted with voluntary bilingualism which is open to those who wish to be bilingual or who wish to work out of their linguistic communities.

At the level of the linguistic divide territorially there should be a distinction between communities and the federated regions along the lines of the Belgium model. Communities will refer to the Anglophone and Francophone entities in global terms while the federated regions will correspond to autonomy areas to be carved out. Such a reform will officially recognize each language in its own sphere while ensuring equality at the centre in the direction of the development we described above. The federalist spirit will have central institutions, federated regional institutions and a skeleton of community institutions. While the central level will look after sovereignty and coordination, the federated regional structures will cater for autonomy issues, all this through power showing mechanisms. The community level which would be partly territorial but essentially cultural will deal principally with issues of specific culture and language. The experience in separate educational systems with the introduction of separate examination boards are a pointers in that direction. The examination boards (GCE Board, *Office du BAC*) could be extended to all steps in the education process to include matters of curriculum, monitoring, pedagogic inspection and examination at all levels from elementary to the tertiary level. As such, one could label this Anglophone or Francophone Community Education Boards with real institutional autonomy. In this regard, some of the competences of the ministerial departments in charge will be transferred to the boards. On will also have a board to deal with Common Law and Civil Law specificities even if the same laws apply to all citizens. The question is whether this will not lead to separatism. Not at all. This is meant for coordination purposes only and better management of diversity. This does not stop every citizen from studying in the other system of each or her choice as is currently the case. It is meant to protect each system of education and culture while allowing possibilities for cross–fertilization. The blurred situation at the moment only leads to confusion. The proposals we are making only go to structure the situation in the direction of better performance.

The university system also has to be restructured in this direction. The distinction in official terms between bilingual universities and monolingual ones leads to a chaotic situation. What goes under the name of bilingual universities operating within the frame of the mother University of Yaoundé far from reflects the label. They simply make for the dwarfing of one language by the other. The problems posed by this type of universities are enormous because a really bilingual university is an ideal. This will imply having personnel to teach every course in the two languages and personnel as well as equipment to translate every course into the other language (either through notes or simultaneous interpretation). This is a real difficulty from the students' point of view that has never been addressed. The challenge for the teacher is to read scripts in a language he/she does not master well. The present situation is chaotic and approximate because of the lack of means to effect the claim. To some students it is simply frustrating.

On the other hand, the problem of completely monolingual universities is that of training monolinguals for a bicultural community. How do we ensure that there is real equity and the reproduction of disparities, inequities and inequalities? The University of Buea has only succeeded in attracting French speaking students who end up graduating because of a rapid intensive language course or the requirement of language proficiency certificate. This has succeeded marvelously well and can be improved upon. The point is that there needs to be a language policy for the universities. One can propose the institution of diploma level second language programmes for candidates who wish to study in a second language any where in the country. In fact, it had worked for Anglophones wishing to study at the Federal University, has worked recently in the University of Buea and works everywhere in the world. This will be a very viable and feasible option. This will entail only more teachers in language teaching and the construction of specialized centres.

Geopolitical Arrangements of a Federal Structure

The novelty in this regard should be a power sharing structure that should seek to solve questions of complexity at three levels: the management of institutions at central level; the specificities of the two linguistic communities structured around the two languages, English and French, and cultures; the problems of internal diversity within the linguistic communities from a geo-economic perspective. A such, the federal level will handle questions of sovereignty and coordination, the community level issues of specific to each component (language, culture, judicial system) and the federated regions problems at that level. This will imply a transfer of competences and means towards the communities and the federated regions with real powers of revenue generation and development initiative. The latter will also possess concrete legislative and executive structures largely independent of the centre. This will be definitely different from the current devolution exercise which goes under the name of decentralization by extending the competences of the federated regions. Besides the federated regions one could also have metropolitan districts with equal powers as the federated regions and having a special status. This is the case of Douala and Yaoundé that merit special attention, the one as a federal capital territory and other as special economic zone. All these have to be discussed within the context of constitutional management that will restructure the country.

The organization of power sharing within the central government will have to be based on quotas as should be nominations into public office. This will reflect communities and federated regions at federal level and sociological composition at federated state level. The logic of balancing only in an ethno–regional direction and to the advantage of the incumbent head of state (as is the current practice) will have to be abolished. Currently, the powers of naming to office are enormous, unchecked, too discretional and makes for abuses. There should be clear and constitutional stipulations about geopolitical sharing of power as opposed to vague arrangements that give wide-ranging powers to the head of state. The current unwritten understanding that creates a balance between Anglophones, Northerners, Centre–South and Coastal peoples is timid and a regression from the 1961-1972 federal constitution which was clear about arrangements at the summit. This definitely needs to change. Constitutional arrangements need to be clear about what quotas go to each community and region in appointments to high official such that any group of people will not feel left out.

Maintaining and Consolidating the Strategic Gains of the Union

These reforms will take place at the same time as there is a need for maintaining, consolidating and perfecting the gains of the union. These are not lacking. The first of these is the idea of a citizenship that is based on equality in rights and obligation. The constitution guarantees this but the risks lies in practices of discrimination or exclusion that are either vestiges of a history that was badly negotiated or attempts to correct other inequalities. One way of further protecting these gains will be to set up sanction systems against any practices that undercut them. The second set of gains consists of the creative blends and the acceptance of specificities of each community (bilingualism, bi-jural nature of the state, educational systems, cultural specificities of each community). Concerning the blends, harmonization should not be limited to a binary vision derived from the construction of identities premised on colonial legacies. They will best function when they are geared at taking the best of each system in the spirit of creative borrowing. The logic should be to work from current exigencies, looking into the past and projecting into the future. The idea is to root the process in the search for solutions to real problems but also looking backward into the past that offered its own solutions as a heritage while having a futuristic vision.

Talking of strategic gains there will be a need to revisit the important transitory clause of the constitution which preserves the legislation carried over from the federal constitution of 1961 – 1972. In fact, Article 68 of the 1996 Revision is clear on this point but it has to go further to restore the clauses which were at the very foundation of the bi- cultural polity. One would be thinking here of those clauses that were categorical on cultural specificity and political autonomy. Realism should dictate an acceptance of the fact that the centralist Jacobin experiment has failed.

The same is very true of attempts to surreptitiously encapsulate the demographically minor partner of the union in the name of national unity and, later on, integration. The last notion itself has been the source of suspicion from the vey beginning and ever since then. "In Southern Cameroonian parlance, *integrated* was definitely a code word for *annexed*" (Ngoh 2011: 75). The failure of any such attempts over tine has led to a rather timid return to specific institution (schools, universities, courts) that reflect the gains of the initial federal character of the union. Rather than accept the inevitable facts and structure them within a constitutional and legal framework, this becomes the substance of politicking where it is the discretion of the prince that dictates when institutions are to be established as when a University was created in Bamenda. It was long overdue for Anglophones to have their own specific universities and professional schools to take care of their needs. The dismantling of specifically Anglophone institutions whether these were of a political, economic, administrative or cultural nature has been detrimental to their collective welfare and has only opened the way for these people to be nearly "swallowed up" (Newns in Ngoh ibid.: 25) as had been predicted before. Whatever the reform process should take, this should be in the spirit of equality, equity and the promise of creative blending that was the very basis of union.

References

Abety, P. "The Literary Podium and Political Pulpit: Medium and Message in Anglophone Drama", *Epasa Moto*, Vol. 1, No. 3, 1996, pp. 250-264.

Ahidjo, A. 1964. *Contributions to National Construction*. Paris : Présence africaine.

Amazee, V. B. Amazee, V.B. "The Myth of Dr. E.M.L. Endeley's Pride in Bongfen Chem-Langhee's 'Southern Cameroons Traditional Authorities and Nationalist Movement, 1953 – 1961'", *Epasa Moto: A Bilingual Journal of Arts, Letters and the Humanities*. Vol. 2, No. 1. 2004, pp. 1-20.
"The German Presence in the British Southern Cameroons, 1922-1946", *South-South Journal of Culture and Development*, Vol. 5, No. 1, June 2003, pp. 145-201.

Ambe, H. "Cameroon Anglophone Theatre as Platform for Reconstructed History and Politics" in P. Fandio and Mongi Madini (eds.) 2007. *Figures de l'Histoire et Imaginaire au Cameroun/Actors of History and Artistic Creativity in Cameroon*. Paris: L'Harmattan, pp. 199-209.

Ambanasom, S. A. "Pedagogy of the Depraved: A Study of the Plays of Victor Epie Ngome, Bole Butake and Bate Besong", *Epasa Moto*, Vol. 1, No. 3, 1996, pp. 218-227.

Amin, S. 1998. Africa and the challenge of Development. Essays. *Ed. by Chris Uroh*. Ibadan: Hope Publications.

"Economic Globalization: Doomed to Break Down" http: www.brettowoodsproject.org/topic/environment/growth/ter7Samin. html.

Amselle, J. – L. 1990. *Logiques métisses. Anthropologie de l'identité en Afrique et ailleurs,* Paris, Payot.

Ateba Yene, T. 1988. *Cameroun, mémoire d'un colonisé*. Paris: L'Harmattan, Collection Mémoires Africaines.

Austen, Ralph A. and Jonathan Derrick. 1999. *Middlemen of the Cameroons River: The Duala and their Hinterland, c.1600 – c.1960*. Cambridge: Cambridge University Press.

Austen, Ralph A. "Mythic Transformation and Historical Continuity: The Duala of Cameroon and German Colonialism, 1884-1914", in I. Fowler and D. Zeitlyn (eds.) 1996. *African Crossroads: Intersections between History and Anthropology in Cameroon*. Providence and Oxford: Berghahn Books, pp. 63-80.

Awasom, N. "Colonial Background to the Development of Autonomist Tendencies in Anglophone Cameroon, 1946-1961", *Journal of Third World Studies*, Vol. 40, No. 1, 1998, pp. 163-183.

"Anglo-Saxonism and Gallicism in Nation-building in Africa: The Case of Bilingual Cameroon and the Senegambia Confederation in Historical Perspective", *Afrika Zamani*, Nos. 11 & 12, 2003-2004, pp. 86-118.

Awasom. Nicodemus A. and Mbu Ettangandop. "The Devolution of Power in the Trust Territories of the Cameroons, 1946 – 1960", *Epasa Moto. A bilingual Journal of Arts, Letters and the Humanities*. Vol. 1, No. 5, 2002, pp. 48-75.

Bayart, J. F. "The neutralization of Anglophone Cameroon" in R. (Ed.) 1978. *Gaullist Africa: Cameroon under Ahmadou Ahidjo*. Enugu Fourth Dimension Publishers, pp. 82-90.
"The birth of the Ahidjo Regime" in R. Joseph (ed.) 1978. *Gaullist Africa: Cameroon under Ahmadou Ahidjo*. Enugu Fourth Dimension Publishers,

Benjamin, J. 1972. *Les Camerounais occidentaux: la minorité dans un état bicommunautaire*. Montréal : Les presses universitaires de Montréal.

Benot, Y. [1994]2001. *Massacres coloniaux. 1944-1950: La IVe République et la mise au pas des colonies françaises*. Paris: La Découverte.

Besong, B. "Literature in the Season of the Diaspora: Notes to the Anglophone Cameroonian writer" in Nalova Lyonga, Eckward

Breitinger, Bole Butake (eds.). 1993. *Anglophone Cameroon Writing.* Bayreuth African Studies Series 30/WEKA, pp. 15-18.

"Ontogenesis of Modern Anglophone Cameroon Drama and its Criticisms", *Voices: The Wisconsin Review of African Languages and Literatures,* Issue 5, Spring 2002, pp. 1-19.

"Nationhood in Dramaturgy: Marginality and Commitment in Victor Epie Ngome's *What God has put asunder"* in P. Fandio and Mongi Madini (eds.) 2007. *Figures de l'Histoire et Imaginaire au Cameroun.* Paris: L'Harmattan, pp. 219-230.

Biyiti bi Essam, J. P. 1984. *Cameroun : complots et bruits de bottes. (Quelques données pour débrouiller l'écheveau).* Paris : Editions l'Harmattan.

Biya, P. 1987. *Communal Liberalism.* Paris: Pierre Marie Favre/ABC; London and Basingstoke: Macmillan Publishers Ltd.

Bourdieu, P. 1994. *Raisons Pratiques : Sur la théorie de l'Action.* Paris : Editions du Seuil.

Bourdieu, P. and L. Wacquant, « Sur les ruses de la raison impérialiste », *Actes de recherche en sciences sociales,* Vol. 121 – 122, 1998, pp. 109 - 118.

Burnham, P. 1996. *The Politics of Cultural Difference in Northern Cameroon.* Edinburgh: Edinburgh University Press.

Chem-Langhëe, B. "The Road to the Unitary State, 1959 – 1972", *Paideuma,* Vol. 41, 1995, pp. 17 -25.

"Anglophone – Francophone Divide and Political Disintegration in Cameroun: a psychosocial perspective", in Nkwi, P.N. and Nyamnjoh, F.B. 1997. *Regional Balance and National Integration in Cameroon: Lessons Learnt and the uncertain Future.* Leiden: African Studies Centre / Yaoundé: International Centre for Applied Social Science and Training (ICASSRT). ICASSRT Monograph No. 1, pp. 88-99.

Courade, C. and G. Courade. 1977. *Education in Anglophone Cameroon*. Yaoundé: ONAREST.

Delancey, M. W. "Plantation and Migration in the Mount Cameroon Region" in Heransgegeben Von Hans F. Illy (ed.) 1972. *Kamerun: Structuren und Probleme der Sozio-ökonominschen entwicklung*. Mainz: v. Hase and Koehler Verlag & Institut für Internationale Solidarität, Der Konrad-Ardenauer-Stiftung. Schriftenreiche BD. 12, pp. 181-235.

De Rohan, J. "L'Identité Transcendée" in Ronan le Coadic (ed.) 2003. *Identités et démocratie. Diversité culturelle et mondialisation: repenser la démocratie*. Rennes : Presses universitaires de Rennes, pp. 11-14.

Derrick, J. "Colonial elitism in Cameroon: the case of the Duala in the 1930s" in M. Njeuma. 1989. *Introduction to the History of Cameroon: Nineteenth and Twentieth Centuries*. London: Macmillan, pp. 106-136.

Dongmo, J. L. "Ethnicité et divergences entre le pouvoir central et les forces vives locales sur la regionalisation au Cameroun. L'exemple du Nord-Cameroun » in Nkwi, P.N. and Nyamnjoh, F.B. 1997. *Regional Balance and National Integration in Cameroon: Lessons Learnt and the uncertain Future*. Leiden: African Studies Centre / Yaoundé: International Centre for Applied Social Science and Training (ICASSRT), ICASSRT Monograph No. 1, pp. 260-279.

Elias, N. 1982. *The Civilising Process*. Oxford: Blackwell. 2 vols.

Epale, S. J. 1975. *Agrarian Capitalism in Western Cameroon, 1885 – 1975: A Case Study in the Modernisation of a Backward Economy*. Unpublished mimeograph.

Feh, Henry Baboh, "Cameroon Legal System", http://www.henrysamuelson.com/index(0-25).html.

Fandio, P."Enseignement des langues étrangères et problématique de l'intégration nationale en Afrique postcoloniale : le cas du Cameroun », *Mots Pluriels*, http :www.arts.uwa.edu.au/MotsPluriels/MP2303pf.html

Fombad, Charles Manga "Researching Cameroonian Law", http://www.nyulawglobal.org/Globalex/Cameroon1.html

Goodridge, R. A. "Activities of Political Organisations: Southern Cameroons, 1945 – 61" in Victor Julius Ngoh. (ed.). 2004. *Cameroon, from a Federal to a Unitary State 1961-1972. A Critical Study.* Limbe: Design House, pp. 13 - 47.

Guibernau, M. 2003. "Entre autonomie et sécession. La prise en compte du nationalisme minoritaire en Catalogne", in Ronan Le Coadic (ed.). *Identités et Démocratie Identités. Diversité culturelle et mondialisation : repenser la mondialisation.* Rennes : Presses universitaires de Rennes, pp. 279-299.

Hobsbawm, E. 1992. "Introduction: Inventing Traditions", in E. Hobsbawm & T. Ranger (eds.), *The Invention of Tradition* (Cambridge-New York-Melbourne: Cambridge University Press), pp.1-14.

Johnson, W. R. 1970. *The Cameroon Federation: Political integration in a fragmentary society.* Princeton: Princeton University Press.

Joseph, R. 1977. *Radical Nationalism in Cameroon: Social origins of the UPC rebellion.* Oxford: Oxford University Press.

Jua, N. "Differential Responses to Disappearing Transitional Pathways: Redefining Possibility among Cameroonian Youths", *African Studies Review,* Vol. 46, No. 2 September 2003, pp. 13-36.

Jua, N. and P. Konings. "Occupation of Public Space. Anglophone Nationalism in Cameroon", *Cahiers d'Etudes africaines,* XLIV (3), 175, 2004, pp. 609 – 633.

Kegne Pokam, E. 1986. *La Problématique de l'unité nationale au Cameroun. Dichotomie entre discours et pratiques dans un système monolithique.* Paris : L'Harmattan.

Kofele-Kale, N. 1980. (ed.). *An African Experiment in Nation-building: The Bilingual Cameroon Republic since Reunification.* Boulder, Colorado: Westview Press.

Konings, P. 1996. "Le « problème anglophone » au Cameroun dans les années 1990" *Politique Afrique,* No. 62, pp. 25-34

"The "Anglophone problem" and chieftaincy in Anglophone Cameroon" in E. Adriaan, B. Van Rouveroy, Van Nieuwaal and Rijk Van Dijk. (eds.) 1999. *African chieftaincy in a new socio-political landscape.* Hamburg: Lit Verlag. Pp. 181-206.

Konings, P. & F. B. Nyamnjoh, "The Anglophone Problem in Cameroon", *The Journal of Modern African Studies*, Vol. 32, No. 2, 1997, pp. 207 – 229.

"Construction and Deconstruction: Anglophones or Autochthones", *The African Anthropologist*, Vol. 7 No. 1, 2000, pp. 5 -32.

2003. *Negotiating an Anglophone Identity: A Study of the Politics of Recognition in Cameroon.* Leiden-London: Brill".

2002. "University Students Revolt, Ethnic militia and Violence during Political Liberalisation in Cameroon" *African studies Review*, Vol. 45, No. 2, pp. 179-204.

Kauzya, J. M. 2001. "A Holistic Model for Managing Ethnic Diversity in the Public Service in Africa", in UNDESA-IIAS, *Managing Diversity in the Civil Service.* Amsterdam-Berlin-Oxford-Tokyo-Washington D.C.: IOS Press, pp. 111 – 121.

Latour, Bruno. *Nous n'avons jamais été modernes. Essai d'anthropologie symétrique.* Paris : La Découverte/Poche.

Levine, V. T. 1964. *The Cameroons from Mandate to Independence.* Berkeley-Los Angeles: University of California Press.

1971. *The Cameroon Federal Republic.* Ithaca/London: Cornell University Press.

Llobera, J. R. 1994. *The God of Modernity: The Development of Nationalism in Western Europe* (Oxford-Dulles: Berg European Studies).

Mamdani, M. 1996. *Citizens and Subjects: contemporary Africa and the Legacy of late colonialism*, Princeton, Princeton University Press.

2001. *When Victims become Killers: Colonialism Nativism and the Genocide in Rwanda.* Kampala: Fountain Publishers; Dar-es- Salaam: E & D Ltd.

Mbassi-Manga, F. 1976. "The State of Contemporary English in Cameroon" in *Cameroon Studies in English and French*, Department of English, University of Yaoundé, Vol. 1, pp. 49-63.

Mbile, N. N. 2000. *Cameroon's Political Story: Memories of an Authentic Eye Witness.* Limbe: Presbyterian Printing Press.

Mbuagbo, Oben Timothy. «Cameroon: Exploiting Anglophone Identity in State Deconstruction", *Social Identities*, Vol. 8, No 3, 2002, pp. 431 – 438.

Melone, S., A. Minkoa She & L. Sindjoun (eds.), *La Réforme constitutionnelle du 18 Janvier 1996 au Cameroun. Aspects juridiques et politiques.* Yaoundé: Association africaine de Science Politique "Section Camerounaise"/ GRAP.

Menthong, H.-L. 1996. "La construction des enjeux locaux dans le débat constitutionnel", in S. Melone, A. Minkoa She & L. Sindjoun (ed.), *La Réforme constitutionnelle du 18 Janvier 1996 au Cameroun. Aspects juridiques et politiques.* Yaoundé: Association africaine de Science Politique "Section Camerounaise"/ GRAP, pp. 146-181.

Mongo Beti. *2003 Main basse sur le Cameroun. Autopsie d'une Colonisation.* Paris : La Découverte.

Morin, Edgar. 1994. *Sociologie.* Paris : Fayard

Mouiche, I. 1997. «Le Royaume Bamoun, les chefferies Bamileke et l'Etat au Cameroun » in Nkwi, P.N. and Nyamnjoh, F.B. 1997. *Regional Balance and National Integration in Cameroon: Lessons Learnt and the uncertain Future.* Leiden: African Studies Centre / Yaoundé: International Centre for Applied Social Science and Training (ICASSRT). ICASSRT Monograph No. 1, pp. 306-322.

Muna, A. "Is OHADA Common Law friendly?" in E. Ngwafor and M. S. Tumnde. 2004. *The Applicability of the OHADA Treaty in Cameroon.* Limbe: Pressprint, pp. 7-16.

Ngamassu, D. "La minorité anglophone au Cameroun: entre l'héritage linguistico-culturel et la construction identitaire", *Traverses: Héritage culturel, élaborations identitaires et langage,* No. 7, 2005, pp. 251-273.

Ngayap, Pierre Flambeau. 1983. *Cameroun: qui gouverne? De Ahidjo à Biya, l'héritage et l'enjeu.* Paris Editions l'Harmattan.

Ngoh, V.J. 1990a. *Cameroun, 1884-1985: Cent Ans d'Histoire.* Yaoundé: Centre d'Edition et de Production pour l'Enseignement et la Recherche (CEPER).

1990b. *Constitutional Developments in Southern Cameroons, 1946-1961: From Trusteeship to Independence.* Yaoundé: Centre d'Edition et de Production pour l'Enseignement et la Recherche.

«The Origins of the Marginalization of former Southern Cameroonians (Anglophones), 1961 -1966: An Historical Analysis", *Journal of Third World Studies,* Vol. XVI, No. 1, 1999, pp. 165-185.

(ed.). 2004. *Cameroon, from a Federal to a Unitary State 1961 – 1972: A Critical Study.* Limbe: Design House.

2011. *The Untold Story of Cameroon Unification: 1955-1961.* Limbe: Pressprint.

Njeuma, Martin Z. "Reunification and Political Opportunism in the Making of Cameroon's independence", *Paideuma,* Vol. 41, pp. 27 – 37.

"Authority, Religion and the Creation of a 'Northern Cameroon' Identity", *Ngaoundéré Anthropos,* Vol. 7, 2002, pp. 32-66.

Nkoum-me-Ntseny, L. –M. 1996a. "Dynamique de positionnement Anglophone et libéralisation politique au Cameroun : de l'identité à l'identification », *Polis: Cameroon Political Science Review,* No. 1, pp. 68 -100.

1996b. «Les 'anglophones' et le processus de l'élaboration de la constitution du 18 janvier 1996 », in S. Melone, A. Minkoa She & L. Sindjoun (dir.), *La Réforme constitutionnelle du 18 Janvier 1996 au Cameroun: aspects juridiques et politiques* (Yaoundé: Association africaine de Science Politique "Section Camerounaise", GRAP), pp. 200 – 2027.

« 'Question anglophone', libéralisation politique et crise de l'état nation » : 'les ennemis dans la maison' », in L. Sindjoun (ed.) 1999. *La Révolution passive au Cameroun : Etat, Société et Changement.* Dakar : Editions Démocraties Africaines, pp. 157 – 229.

Nkwi, P. N. and Nyamnjoh, F.B. 1997. *Regional Balance and National Integration in Cameroon: Lessons Learnt and the uncertain Future.* Leiden: African Studies Centre/Yaoundé: International Centre for Applied Social Science and Training (ICASSRT). ICASSRT Monograph No. 1.

Nyamnjoh, F. B. 1996. *The Cameroon G. C. E. Crisis: A Test of Anglophone Solidarity.* Limbe: Nooremac.

1997. "Anglophone Liberation Journalism and National Deconstruction in Cameroon" in Nkwi, P.N. and Nyamnjoh, F.B. 1997. *Regional Balance and National Integration in Cameroon: Lessons Learnt and the uncertain Future.* Leiden: African Studies Centre / Yaoundé: International Centre for Applied Social Science and Training (ICASSRT). ICASSRT Monograph No. 1, pp. 67-78.

1999. "Cameroon: A country united by Ethnic Ambition and Differences." *African Affairs: The Journal of the Royal African Society,* Vol. 98, No. 390 January 1999, pp. 101-109.

Nyerere, J. 1966. *Freedom and Unity: A Selection of Speeches and Writings.* Dar es Salaam: Oxford University Press.

Olinga, A. D. «La 'question anglophone' dans le Cameroun d'aujourd'hui», *Revue juridique et politique,* Vol. 3, pp. 292-308.

Rivière, C. 2000. *Anthropologie politique.* Paris : Armand Colin.

Savidan, P. "La reconnaissance des identités culturelles comme enjeu démocratique » in Rohan le Coadic (ed.) 2003. *Identités et démocratie.Diversité culturelle et mondialisation: repenser la démocratie.* Rennes : Presses universitaires de Rennes, pp. 231 - 253.

Sindjoun, L. 1996. "L'imagination constitutionnelle de la Nation" in S. Melone, A. Minkoa She & L. Sindjoun (dir.), *La Réforme constitutionnelle du 18 Janvier 1996 au Cameroun: aspects juridiques et politiques* (Yaoundé: Association africaine de Science Politique "Section Camerounaise", GRAP), pp. 200-227.

Tchombe, T. 2001. "Structural Reforms in Education in Cameroon", http:www.unifr.ch/ipg/ecodoc/conferences/DocuPDF-Conf-Inter/Tchombe.pdf.

Tatah Mentan, E. "Constitutionalism, Press and Factional Politics. Coverage of Sawa Minority Agitations in Cameroon". Melone, S., A. Minkoa She and L. Sindjoun (ed.). 1996. *Le Reforme Constitutionnelle du 18 Janvier 1996. Aspects Juridiques et Politiques.* Yaoundé : Fondation Fredrich Ebert and Association Africaine de Science Politique (Section Camerounaise)/ GRAP, pp. 182-198.

Tumnde, M. S. "The Applicability of the OHADA Treaty in Cameroon: Problems and Prospects" in E. Ngwafor and M. S. Tumnde (eds.). 2004. *The Applicability of the OHADA Treaty in Cameroon.* Limbe: Pressprint, pp. 42-53.

Wonyu Engène. 1985. *De l'UPC à l'UC: témoignage à l'aube de l'indépendance (1953 – 1961).* Paris: Harmattan.

Wievorka, M. 2001. *La Différence.* Paris : Balland.
2010. *Neuf Leçons de Sociologie.* Paris: éditions Robert Laffont (Pluriel).

Yenshu Vubo, E. "Balanced Rural Development in Cameroon within a Democratic Context" in Nkwi, P.N. and Nyamnjoh, F.B. (eds.). 1997. *Regional Balance and National Integration in Cameroon: Lessons Learnt and the uncertain Future.* Leiden: African Studies Centre / Yaoundé: International Centre for Applied Social Science and Training (ICASSRT). ICASSRT Monograph No. 1, pp. 129-137.

"The Discourse and Polities of Indigenous /minority People's Right in some Metropolitan Areas of Cameroon" *Journal of Applied Social Sciences*, Vol. 1, No. 1, 1998, pp. 25-41.

"Levels of Historical Awareness. The Development of Identity and Ethnicity in Cameroon", *Cahiers d'Etudes Africaines*, Vol. 43, No. 3, 2003, pp. 591-628.

"The Management of Ethnic Diversity in Cameroon: The Coastal Areas" in Fomin, E.S.D. and Forje, J. W. (eds.). 2005. *Central Africa: Crises and Reform*. Dakar: CODESRIA Books, pp. 41-63.

"Management of Ethnic Diversity in Cameroon against the backdrop of social crises», *Cahiers d'Etudes Africaines,* Vol, 46, No. 1, 2006, pp. 135 – 15.

"L'intelligentsia camerounaise entre nationalisme radical, nationalisme à basse intensité et dérive sectariste», in Abel Kouvouama, Abdoulaye Gueye, Anne Piriou and Anne-Catherine Wagner (eds.), 2007, *Figures croisées d'intellectuels :trajectoires, modes d'action, productions*, Paris, Karthala.

2009. *Tradition et Modernité au Cameroun. Autour de la Transethnicité*. Mémoire d'Habilitation à Diriger des Recherches. Besançon: Université de Franche-Comté.

Yenshu Vubo E. and George A. Ngwa. "Changing Intercommunity Relations and the Politics of Identity in the Northern Mezam Cameroon Area", *Cahiers d'Etudes Africaines*, Vol. 41, N° 1, 2001, pp. 163-190.

Appendix I

Reflections on Changing Times: Political Obstinacy, Legacies and the Anglophone Problem (Being a series of newspaper articles that appeared in *The Post* newspaper October and November 2000)

Politics in some parts of the South has earned for itself the tag of a "dirty game". One would not be idealising to say that competitive politics based on popular sovereignty has reached a stage of refinement in the North. Proof of this is the willingness of politicians to step down when confronted with a vote of no confidence, a scandal, the loss of popularity or failure to win elections. There is a dirty side, true, but this left in the dark, in those domains out of the glaring eye of the electorate. This is not the same in the South where politicians do not care to observe the tides and are willing to use force or guile to cling to power, force the course of events or push an idea through. The difference in the two political attitudes is that one is based on realistic political analysis and objective values such as patriotism while the second is based on the egoistic tendency to win at all course even against the odds. This attitude, which I choose to term political obstinacy, is accompanied by acts such as the refusal to accept defeat, election rigging, the use of force to achieve objectives (hiring of thugs, violence), deceiving the electorate, taking advantage of an innocent and ignorant electorate, rejection of compromise and corruption.

The consequence of this type of political behaviour is popular disenchantment with politics, elector apathy and the initiation of a cycle of vice (witness the maxim: violence begets violence). The present reflections will take as example the question of the territory and people of the Northwest and Southwest Provinces of the Republic of Cameroon, once administered by the British under a league of Nations and the United Nations mandates as Southern Cameroons and which existed for eleven years as the Federated State of West Cameroon within the context of a federal experiment.

The question we are going to answer here is that of the cause of the malaise which has been referred to as the Anglophone question. Although many reasons have been advanced to account for this malaise namely, the naively, low level of education of English speaking politicians, the Machiavellian attitude of Mr. Ahidjo and his successor, internecine disputes amongst Anglophone politicians and the demographic, intellectual and economic imbalances between the negotiating parties at independence, our hypothesis is that these are contributing factors but not sufficient enough to explain the turn of events. Our contention is that the main factor that has contributed to the present crisis that is known as the Anglophone question is the style of politics we have described above as obstinate politics. We will examine this style of politics and its relation, its consequences or the present crisis and the possibilities for solutions.

Predictable Outcomes of Obstinate Politics: The Difficulties of the Cameroon's Options and Politics of Independence

If there is a controversy over the status of the English speaking people in Cameroon today, this was predictable looking at the style of politics that characterized the transition process. It was marked by insincerity, falsehood and manipulation. I will recount some of the instances that have either been reported in print or still form part of the memory of some of the actors.

In order to prove that they had been maltreated in the Nigerian Eastern House of Assembly, the KNC group brought stones to show their people that they had been chased away. Geologists may bear me out but what difference is there between Enugu stones and those of Mamfe for instance?

There is apparently no plausible reason why late Dr. Foncha's faction broke away from the KNC to form an independent political movement if not for selfish reasons. This is evidently the germ of the so-called Northwest/Southwest divide and its consequent regional politics. This put a deep divide in the English speaking delegation during the negotiations.

Objectively there was no reason why late Foncha's KNDP group opted to join French Cameroons. It is true that transfrontier peoples existed (e.g. Douala-Bakweri, Dschang-Fontem, Bamboutos-Ngemba, Bakossi-Mbo Bakaka) but the same situation can also be observed across the Southern Cameroon-Nigerian border. On the contrary, the independence war in French Cameroon and the linguistic barrier was a security deterrent that could have militated against such an option.

The KNDP campaigns during the 1961 were based on deceit and manipulation. Examples of lies: The then Prime Minister, Dr. EML Endeley had handed his bag to the Fon of Bali Nyonga during the London talks. PM Endeley was going to pose Fons. The issue was simply secession from Nigerian. It is now an established fact that there was a heavy disappointment when the majority only discovered after the elections that victory meant unification with La République du Cameroun (as my SCNC friends religiously call French Cameroon of the period).

The incumbent transitional government is reported to have heavily rigged the plebiscite elections and it is also common knowledge that the administering power (UN via UK) turned a blind eye to these abuses. Declassified documents will surely bear us out today. The principal question which remains to be answered is whether it was absolutely necessary to rig elections when one had inherited power through a democratic process. Proof of this attitude of winning at all cost against all evidence is the fact that areas such as Wum, Nkambe, Banso, Babanki which voted for the KNC in KNDP majority areas were victimized (chiefs flogged or sent into exile, development blocked etc).

There was extensive manipulation of traditional civil society organizations and status holders against the KNC and in favour of the KNDP. The *anlu* and *fombuen* (all traditional women's organizations in Kom, Babanki, Oku and related areas) were indoctrinated in hate style against all KNC politicians. For instance, in Kom it was widely circulated amongst women that Endeley's KNC government was planning to alienate land to the Ibo and change age-old farming methods by force. Women stood up for a cause whose logic they were largely ignorant of but whose gains were purely political and unrelated to what was really their own concerns.

Chiefs were also briefed with half truths to mobilize a population largely unaware of the issues at stake. They themselves held views which were diametrically opposed to those of the KNDP.

On both side of the 1916 divide only pro-communist elements, who were either not in mainstream politics (UPC) or were in the minority (OK), championed the idea of unification. By all counts the idea was not central to politics until the violence of the UPC and the intrigues of the OK forced the UC and the KNDP, who wanted to win at all cost, to adopt it albeit reluctantly. It was therefore out of opportunism that reunification was forced through. Politicians will tell you this is expedience or pragmatism (sic). Really Machiavellian to run on a platform you do not believe in simply because it is a winning idea.

Listen to the most ridiculous of ideas: Endeley's idea was not good because his wife was Nigerian as if when one is a politician one should not marry across borders. Really cheap talk. I hope they were married to French Cameroonians to canvas for joining them. This idea should not have been aching today but for the fact that some of our elderly statesmen go over national television and utter this without thinking and without any editing. I think they should examine themselves and state in all honesty that they did not have the better option after they "won". Anyway, the obstinacy has stayed on simply because they want to cling on to the "fame". It would surprise me because they make contradictory utterances all over the place and in completely opposed camps. At one time, they are found to be trying to "white wash" themselves in "illegal" meetings and at others trying to play safe.

The KNDP argument that the Ibos presence in Southern Cameroons was domineering was a good argument for the achievement of internal autonomy in 1958, but beyond that there was a need for the transitional internal government to undertake reforms to translate into concrete reality this achievement. In fact, between 1955 and 1961 there are no recorded reforms that tended to protect the citizens within the context of the internal autonomy. On the contrary, much effort was wasted in the "politics of winning" rather than trying to consolidate what had been won. To continue to brandish this argument at the dawn of independence showed that the KNDP underrated the achievement. From all counts there was no objective reason to have adopted the French Cameroons option of the two alternatives. On the contrary, the Nigerian options had some positive side which could have been considered by the major parties in competition.

First the option of full autonomy on equal status with the other major regions (East, West, North) was an asset which could have been exploited positively by the elite to protect area from the domination of the Eastern Region, and in fact all the other Regions of the Federation. It was proof of political myopia to have left this option for no better alternative or an alternative to be negotiated. Where did our "heroes" keep the saying that a bird in band is worth two in the bush? Nigerian (in the main Ibo) domination could be considered an epiphenomenon that could have with been warded off with the achievement of autonomy.

Secondly, the cultural factor was in fact seriously and blindly underestimated. The Nigerian option made for continuity with an English speaking people, whose rudiments, the Southern Cameroons had been introduced into. I refer to rudiments because, contrary to some propagandists, one cannot talk of a cultural heritage inherited from the British who had been economical enough not to invest culturally in the territory. In fact the former was content to leave education at elementary level and whatever culture that is British has been learnt either within the experimental federal Republic (Parliamentary Procedures, Community Development, Education, etc), within the Unitary state or in continuous cultural association/dependence on Nigeria. The latter point is capital, and often overlooked, but is a serious pointer to the error of the independence politicians. If one examines the curriculum of primary education up till the 1970s, one will find that it was still modelled on the Nigerian system. Even after text books based on the metric system were introduced in the early1970s they were still being used side-by-side with Nigerian text books. Nigerian literature continued to be in circulation and has only rather progressively reduced than totally replaced.

The most important of the cultural factors is its finest aspect, university education. It is common knowledge that there were only two important options left to Anglophone Cameroonians who could not afford the fee or achieve a scholarship to study in Europe and North America. These were namely the University of Yaoundé, and Nigerian Universities. The latter option was more appealing to most members of the middle class who could afford the fees and living expenses, while the former came only as a last option or the "pauper's option". The consequence is that a sizeable proportion of the English speaking elite have been trained in Nigeria while a minority was either trained at the lone University of Yaoundé or in so-called professional schools. As a graduate of University of Yaoundé, I can bet that it was not an easy task, this characterized for the most time by deep frustration, resentment and at times conflict. In fact, success came only as a challenge. I cannot say that there were no success stories. There were, and even spectacular ones like myself, but they were the exception and not the rule. I have even often tended to consider the Anglophone students who studied in the University of Yaoundé as the guinea pigs of the Unification Experiment because unlike the experiment in bilingual education in Molyko-Buea and the Teacher Training Practicing Schools, the Yaoundé experience consisted, in most cases, in mental brutalisation. Or else how could one explain that students who had been trained only in English be suddenly obliged to study in a second language without prior initiation into that language in the name of bilingualism? The experience could best be described as a nightmare, wasting and destroying in many cases many of the best Cameroonian brains in the process. I am not saying that Francophone Cameroonians did not find things difficult but theirs can be considered an academic problem per se while the Anglophones faced but a cultural problem that came only to compound the academic one.

When it comes to integration into the job market, it may be difficult to say exactly what the experience has been. However, English-speaking Cameroonians who studied in English speaking countries have faced problems of integrating into a society which ought to be theirs. The most important problem is that of the equivalence of degrees. It is important to have comparable scales of measurement of certificates but the purpose is defeated when people have to wait till eternity to be told the level to which they belong. On the contrary, it is stupid to seek to absolutely equate degrees, when it is common knowledge that the worth of certificates depends on awarding universities and the practical value of the certificate.

The ultimate consequence of this situation is that within the elite of English speaking extraction, there has arisen both a complex and a rift between the integrated and un-integrated which is at the heart of the present crisis. There is a complex of superiority and a feeling of frustration among English speaking Cameroonians who studied in universities out of the country. The complex of superiority arises from the belief in the inherent superiority of an English speaking culture, and hence, a qualification clumsily called Anglo-Saxon culture. By the way, the term Anglo-Saxon is either an ethnic term in the American (USA) context to mean totally different things or a French term to refer to the English speaking world of Germanic extraction. This has given use to a snobbish attitude towards all degrees earned at the University of Yaoundé and the other schools of Higher learning.

There is also frustration because these elite cannot integrate into the mainstream of the Cameroon culture or work force. The argument I am making is that these are evident errors which could have been avoided if the integration-with- Nigeria option was adopted. There was no reason why Endeley and Foncha should have been obligatorily opposed on the option to choose. Was it not possible to champion the same cause against unification. I still feel strongly that Foncha's adoption of the unification was not objective motivated.

The Present Crisis and the Possibilities

Whatever the case the situation is totally different today as English speaking Cameroonians having taken a very long and independent journey with the French speaking Cameroonians with all the problems associated with it. It is necessary to look at the objective conditions today and build on them rather than resort to the same obstinate politics of the independence years. What one observes today is a replica of the latter. It is necessary that the government musters all its force to prove that there is no 'Anglophone' problem, or that the SCNC should opt out totally from the union? Is it not possible to look at the objective conditions of cohabitation or common national life, highlighting the achievements and merits of the experiment problems, the prospects and the solutions to the problems rather than striving to prove that all is rosy or that nothing works as both government agents and the SCNC are doing?

Although this dream has not been realized it is still a lively dream which is sustained by many who are making it work, despite the problems. If it is not working its because of obstinacy continues to characterise the attitudes of some people within the union. The many who think it can work are building on the possibilities that exist. I wish to look at some of these possibilities or entry points that have made this experiment to work before looking at what remains to be achieved.

First, we can refer to the partial integration of English speaking elite. Although this can be taken as negative since it does not give the possibility to everybody to be integrated, it is the first proof of the fact that the experiment is possible.

Secondly, two events have enhanced the image and status of the English speaking Cameroonian in Cameroon in the last ten years, namely the emergence of the SDF as a political force and the creation of the University of Buea. For the first time in four decades of common existence, English speaking Cameroonians were in a position to prove themselves to their compatriots and attract a voluntary following in the French speaking community. In fact, some obstinate politicians think that the SDF leadership has been taken hostage by its French speaking elite while French speaking candidates are invading the University of Buea. On the contrary, I think that these developments are an asset to English speaking Cameroonians and the nation building experience, and thus have to be taken seriously. While the SDF has enhanced the direct participation of the English speaking community in public affairs, the University of Buea has become the model of University education in Cameroon. This should not be underestimated.

Thirdly, the English speaking community has come to be perceived as one of the normal components of national life in Cameroon. In all the urban areas in the predominantly French speaking community, they have their place alongside others, with places for their own schools, businesses, churches and social activities in respect of their specific culture. The blue-shirt-khaki-shorts uniform of the English speaking Cameroonian has ceased from being an insult to become an object of a people's pride. I do not need to indicate that where Anglophones live in the French speaking side of Cameroon, one will find a primary school, an English speaking parish of the Roman Catholic Church, parishes of the PCC or CBC and even Pentecostal churches. Some Anglophone Cameroonians have very colossal businesses in Douala, Yaoundé and Bafoussam (where the opportunities exist) to the extent that separatism will constitute a danger to their interests.

In as much as we can build on these irreversible achievements by improving on them and by enlarging their scope, there are still some areas of deep discontent that need to be addressed for English speaking Cameroonians to move forward. A lot has been written about these issues and it will be useless highlighting all of them here. I will point to some which I consider to be crucial. The first of these is the inherent belief in some French speaking Cameroonians that English speaking Cameroonian will only hold a secondary position in political or administrative office. This is deeply entrenched such that it has come to be an unwritten law or connivance between all French speaking politicians that is tacitly accepted by the English speaking elite. A change of this mentality will not be easy. But the hope will lie in the present generation of English and French speaking Cameroonians who are living, studying and working together.

Appendix II

Academic Honours for Dr Temngah Joseph Nyambo of the University Of Douala

The Representative of the Minister of Higher Education
The Rector of the University of Douala
Colleagues
Dear mourners

It is painful to stand here today to bear testimony to the works of a friend who was everything to me. He was a brother in every true sense of the word to the extent that everybody that knew him associated me with him or him with me. It is not painful that he died because he died. It is rather painful that he died so young. Dying so young for a talented man like Joe – as he was fondly called by everybody – is painful because the world will surely miss his best qualities that I am here to present. I would have wished that when two of us would have given the best of ourselves to the world we would have died in natural succession and he would have been the one to talk about my own works, he being slightly younger than me. Unfortunately for me that is not the way of the law of death. If I stand here today to give a testimony of my bosom friend's life works it is precisely because we have gone a long way as friends. Two of us had learnt to be true apostles of the academia and had learnt to live to that culture although coming from two different paths, namely Law for him and Sociology for me. I met Joe through a common friend in the 1980s when he was an undergraduate student and I was a post graduate student at the then University of Yaoundé. By sharing our common problems as students and having an exciting time as youngsters we came to know and respect each other. Above all we came to be real pals because we shared the same intellectual dispositions. That is what came to seal our bonds to the extent that we became soul brothers. What everybody should know is that these bonds were strengthened by a certain extreme form of mutual respect that I have not found in the friends that I have made before or that rarely exists in the intellectual community. In the process of our friendship I tried as much as possible to play the elder brother role. For example, when everybody was affirming that the Doctorat de Troisième cycle was a lengthy waste of time or impossible, I proved to him that it was possible by going through it in 1991. After that I advised him to continue which he did defend in 1995. In that regard he followed my lead and became a university lecturer like myself after he defended that degree. In his professional life he tried as much as possible to follow my advice and as God would have it his fortunes were similar to mine. He was called to build the new Department of Common Law tradition in the University of Douala from the year 2000 in the same year as I was made Head of Department of Sociology and Anthropology in the University of Buea. We shared in our intellectual pursuits and learnt from each other. I learnt a lot of Law and Jurisprudence from Dr Temngah as he learnt a lot of Sociology and Anthropology from me. One can see that Sociology and Anthropology running through his works as the Law and Jurisprudence in my analysis. Although he pursued his independent career I tried to involve him in anything that could have a relation to his research interests. I will come back to that later. We shared the same political interests and tried to find a place for ourselves in the evolving political landscape throughout the shaky transition process in the country. When we became too immersed in our academic pursuits this political interests became less intense but shifted in the same direction: career. I have very few true friends. I have lost one. I have to pay him the homage that is befitting.

Dr Temngah Joseph Nyamboh was born on 10 May 1966 at Mumfu in Menchum Division. He studied in the Presbyterian Boy's School Victoria (to later become Limbe) from 1974 to 1976 and Government School Abar – Misong Menchum Division from 1976 to 1979 when he terminated his primary education. His had his secondary education at the New Era Institute from 1980 to 1984 (for the First Cycle) and Government High School, Limbe from 1984 to 1986 (for the Second Cycle). He attended the Faculty of Laws of Laws and Economics of the then University of Yaoundé from 1986 – 1993 where he obtained the Licence and the Maîtrise en Droit and then the newly created University of Yaoundé II from 1993 till 1995 when he completed the Doctorat de Troisième Cycle that he had started in the old University before the 1993 reforms.

The works of Dr Temngah span a variety of sub-fields of Law: Labour Law, Trade Unionism, Customary Law, Human Rights, Family Law (Widowhood, Adoption), International Law (harmonisation processes) and Jurisprudence. As a scholar Dr Temngah tried to emulate the pioneer generation of Cameroonian intellectuals and one could see this transpire through his works. His theses, articles and library reflected this. In order to be a genuine academic (not to use the term intellectual) he was addicted to reading and collected books, newspapers and journals from a wide range of disciplines. When we went through his library when he was still alive one would not be surprised to find books in disciplines far removed from his original Law. To him I saw that a scholar was first and foremost a reader. To stimulate his mind and to be able to comment on facts of legal importance one had to be acquainted with the most diverse of facts whether these were historical, social or medical. It is in this regard that he presented the image of a living encyclopaedia of the social and political facts of Cameroon and was the best person with whom to work on projects concerning the country. We even embarked on a common project of forming an association which only his political acumen could get legalised.

I will like us to look at the themes that Dr Temngah treated in his works and how these constituted major contributions in his field. As I understand him labour law and trade unionism were his major preoccupations. These were the domains which constituted the thrust of his Doctorat de Troisième Cycle thesis, some published articles and a Doctorat d'Etat thesis he had submitted to the Faculty of Laws of the University of Yaoundé II. It is also on this basis that I commissioned him to write a chapter on the history of trade unionism as part of a book on *Civil Society and the Search for Development Initiatives in Cameroon* (to be published by CODESRIA this year). His analysis of the protection of the right to work in Cameroon poses the question of how legislation that protects the right to work translates into the reality of having and effectively enjoying work. It is in this work that we find an emerging interest in articulating levels of analysis between national and international levels of legislation. If an international organisation such as the ILO makes it an obligation for member countries to ensure that citizens of a country have the right to work and the country ratifies this international legislation by adopting laws that are in consonance with this line of thought how does this become reality? Dr Temngah lays the groundwork for what will become his major intellectual preoccupation by showing the difficulties attendant on harmonising local legislation and imperatives arising from international obligations. It is within the scope of this work that we find this articulate intellectual trace the role of trade unionism as an instrument of protecting workers' rights. This work has resulted in one class A journal articles ("Remedies for Wrongful Dismissal" *African Journal of International and Comparative Law*), one article in the *Annals of the Faculty of Letters of the University of Douala* ("Trade Unionism in Cameroon: From Autonomy to State Controlled"), and a contribution towards the CODESRIA sponsored book that I coordinated and edited that is still in press ("The Evolution of Trade Unionism and the Prospects for Alternatives to the Labour Question in Cameroon" *Civil Society and the Search for Development Alternatives in Cameroon* [published 2008]). He continued his research from where he left the Doctorat de Troisième Cycle and was going to crown it with a Doctorat d'Etat on the topic *The International Labour Organisation and the Implementation of Human Rights in Africa: the case of Cameroon* when he was snatched prematurely by the cold hands of death.

Dr. Temngah's preoccupation with customary law derives from his initial preoccupation with issues of the family which remains largely governed in practice by so-called native laws and customs. His inaugural work in this regard is his Maîtrise mémoire which to my judgment equalled any Master's degree thesis. It will surprise any person in this audience to note that this mémoire has been at the basis of 2 class A journal articles, one with the *Revue Générale de Droit* of the University of Ottawa and another with the *African journal of International and Comparative Law* as well as one other article in the Annals of the Faculty of Laws and Political Science of the University of Dschang. It is emblematic that he started his reflections and investigations in that regard with the most problematic and troubling aspects of family life: widowhood. In his mémoire he tries to analyse the complications of the entrapment of widowhood practices in custom when in terms of statutory law there are provisions for protection of widows. He comes back to this question when he examines the place of women's rights in general vis-à-vis customary and statutory law in the article "Customary Law, Women's Rights and Traditional Courts in Cameroon" in the *Revue Générale de Droit* and the more recent article "Female Inheritance between Customary Law and Modern Jurisprudence" presented to the journal *Terroirs*. Throughout, he is worried about the seeming contradictions between customary law and received laws found in our statutes. This comes out again in the article "Adoption of children under customary and statutory law in Cameroon: Need for Unification" in the *Africa Journal of International and Comparative Law* Vol. 9, No. 4. Rather than being dismissive in the manner of modernists whose embracing of statutory law against custom has no other justification than the adoption of fashion, Dr. Temngah has always felt that there is a need to rationally integrate aspects of customary law in the laws of the country. This, he argues, goes beyond the two dimensional preoccupation with harmonizing received legal practices obtaining in the bi-jural context of Civil Law (French) and Common Law (English) to embrace customs and international law which is constantly becoming an imperative aspect of jurisprudence in the age of so-called globalisation. He comes back to this very often and argues strongly for a process of codification as the best way towards harmonization. It is in this regard that Temngah distinguishes himself from most Cameroonian intellectuals who take refuge in the easy argument of the cultural war between Anglophones and Francophones to whom the ultimate reality of living in the bicultural experience of Cameroon is cultural incompatibility.

This should be because Joe embraced the idea of the project of a united Cameroon nation in its diversity as worthwhile. To him and me we believed (and I still believe and will do him the honour to believe) that the project of a Cameroon nation is exciting, colourful and unique. Before his untimely and shocking death we had discussed the project of co-authoring a book on the bi-jural experience of Cameroon. I had already proposed a draft whose typed copy he was supposed to complement with his knowledge of the legal and political history of Cameroon. I had discussed the main ideas with him as well as other colleagues such as late Dr Etienne Njiki Bikoi of the University of Buea. Today I find myself alone with such a project that will surely lack their inputs. The only way to pay them true honour is to finish the book and dedicate it to them.

In a tradition that has almost become entrenched in Cameroon's academic culture and which makes of all of us some sort of players of variety music, Dr Temngah also delved into a wide variety of legal issues. Besides providing a chapter on the legal framework of civil society in the forthcoming volume on *Civil Society and the Search for Development Alternatives in Cameroon,* Dr Temngah also published several articles and presented communications to diverse forums in domains not directly related to the areas which his graduate research had led him to. If death had allowed him the normal life span of the psalmist ("three score and ten or by reason of strength four score" Psalm 90), we would have had more than this. Let us say that he had just opened the way. Above all I have to underline the fact that his life works are a testimony to the fact that one can have good degrees in Cameroon and put them into value at any level.

Dr. Temngah's colleagues of Yaoundé II Soa, Ngaoundéré and Douala are definitely best placed to dwell on the teaching aspect of his career. It will suffice it for me to make a few comments on this dimension from an institutional and political perspective. My friend was a young and dynamic actor in expanding the world of learning in the domain of Common Law whose department he was called to head in the University of Douala and by offering his expertise to the sister University of Ngaoundéré, the College of Administration and Magistracy (ENAM) and the Regional Centre for Labour Administration (CRADAT), Yaoundé. To some people this may appear obvious. What we had agreed on in our discussions was that university studies in Cameroon have been dominantly in French and from a French perspective. The structure of the former University of Yaoundé and the new universities in French-speaking Cameroon attest to this. The creation of a university of English expression is good but not the best. People like Joseph Temngah have not only continued to teach in the predominantly French milieu; they have also decided to expand and consolidate studies in English and about English culture there. Dr. Temngah decided to take the challenge to do what mostly the more senior academics were doing: set up a new Department and pilot it with zeal. In the English speaking traditions of academia, departmental chairs are the summit of professional life. It is a prestige to animate a unit of such magnitude and to give direction and leadership. To pioneer one such unit and to give it a place and meaning is a land mark. I will call on all colleagues of his Department and faculty to continue to build on this idea, dwelling on the positive side and consolidating the strides of the Department during his stewardship. As for his shortcomings they are important because correcting them will only strengthen the Department.

I have the strong feeling from observation that the interest in interdisciplinary interactions and friendship that Dr. Temngah had with me that he also shared same with many colleagues across disciplines in Douala. I have come across many colleagues who were in the same position (like me) with my bosom friend. The collapsing of the sharp disciplinary boundaries is a virtue that we should promote. Specialisation – even in its extreme form – is a reality of modern academic life but the imperative of cross–fertilization is more imperative than ever before. In its social dimension it is the spice of conviviality on campuses. My friend and colleague is no more but we must keep up the flame of the conviviality because it is good in itself. Now we need to do that in his honour

There are a few promises that I can personally make to the world. The first is to ensure that the uncompleted publications projects are finalized. The second is to federate as many people as possible to our common ideals and around his budding ideas which were still to find full expression. I had floated the idea of a *Society, History and Economy Forum* to him and he was excited about it. Why not make it a reality for him? Why not revive the association which we started when we were still in Yaoundé? That is my personal commitment. I will only call on mourners to strive to gain inspiration from this much that he did to the best of his abilities. His Department and Faculty, his friends and students will surely do him justice in continuing in the pioneering path that he traced. On a personal note I will appeal that we stand by Dr. Temngah's family and give them the support that they need to go through these difficult times. Let us also forgive him in our deepest of hearts and rehabilitate him where he failed.

Good bye dear friend. You have left me alone and gone to return no more. I will live to keep memories of our times together that suffered no strain whatsoever. The only strain is your having left me so soon to face the vicissitudes of this world alone. Adieu.

Emmanuel Yenshu Vubo
Senior Lecturer, University of Buea

www.ingramcontent.com/pod-product-compliance
Lightning Source LLC
Chambersburg PA
CBHW022228010526
44113CB00033B/646